The Egypt Exploration Society

- the early years

Sixteenth Occasional Publication

The Egypt Exploration Society

- the early years

Edited by
Patricia Spencer

The Egypt Exploration Society
3 Doughty Mews
London WC1N 2PG
2007

LONDON

SOLD AT THE OFFICES OF THE EGYPT EXPLORATION SOCIETY
3 DOUGHTY MEWS, LONDON WC1N 2PG
www.ees.ac.uk

AND BY

OXBOW BOOKS
10 HYTHE BRIDGE STREET
OXFORD OX1 2EW, UK
and
THE DAVID BROWN BOOK CO
PO BOX 511 (28 MAIN STREET)
OAKVILLE, CT 06779, USA
www.oxbowbooks.com

A catalogue for this book is available from the British Library

ISBN 978 0 85698 185 2

Set in Adobe InDesign CS2 by Patricia Spencer

The SymbolGreek II font used in this work is available from Linguist's Software, Inc.,
PO Box 580, Edmonds, WA 98020-0580, USA. Phone: + 1 425 775-1130. www.linguistsoftware.com

Printed in Great Britain by Commercial Colour Press plc,
Angard House, 185 Forest Road, Hainault, Essex IG6 3HU. www.ccpress.co.uk

Contents

Preface and Acknowledgements

In 1982, when the Egypt Exploration Society celebrated its centenary, a history of the Society was published by the British Museum Press, to coincide with a successful exhibition at the Museum about the Society's first century of work in Egypt. Edited by T G H James, *Excavating in Egypt. The Egypt Exploration Society 1882-1982* has long been out of print and when the Society's 125th anniversary was approaching Mr Paul Sussman suggested that to mark the occasion a companion volume should be published which would rely more heavily on images from the Society's extensive Archive which contains the records of 125 years of work in Egypt and Sudan. It was decided for the Anniversary volume to concentrate on the Society's early years, between its foundation in 1882 and the First World War, leaving open the option, if this book is well-received, of succeeding volumes on the Society's later work.

Virtually all of the images included come from the Society's Lucy Gura Archive, held at the London premises, but some have generously been provided by the Petrie Museum of Egyptian Archaeology, University College London, the Griffith Institute, Oxford and by the Papyrology Rooms in the Sackler Library at the Ashmolean Museum, Oxford. The Society is very grateful to Dr Stephen Quirke and Ms Janet Picton at the Petrie Museum, Dr Jaromir Malek at the Griffith Institute and Dr Dirk Obbink at the Oxford Papyrology Rooms for their help in ensuring the widest possible coverage of excavations undertaken by the Society in these early years.

Thanks are also due to The Bodleian Library, University of Oxford for permission to reproduce the image of P. Oxy I, 1 on page 227 and to the following who scanned images for inclusion in the book: Dr Andrew Bednarski, Dr Nikolaos Gonis, Mr Christopher Naunton, Ms Janet Picton and Dr Jeffrey Spencer.

Mr Paul Sussman and Mr Christopher Naunton have been involved with the design and production of the book from the start and have provided invaluable assistance with editing and proofreading. The Society is also grateful to Mr Naunton for compiling the Bibliography and to Dr Aidan Dodson who kindly provided the map showing most of the sites mentioned in the book.

Rendering Egyptian Arabic place names in English is always a challenge, as so many variants exist in different publications and it is almost impossible to reach a consensus on the 'correct' forms. For this book it has been decided, therefore, to use the spellings current at the time of the work and used in the relevant contemporary EEF publications.

The Society now has an ongoing project to digitise, document fully and rehouse as much of its Archive as possible (see further p.255). This project was initiated in this Anniversary year by a generous donation from the estate of a member, Miss Lucy Gura, after whom the Archive has now been named.

Patricia Spencer

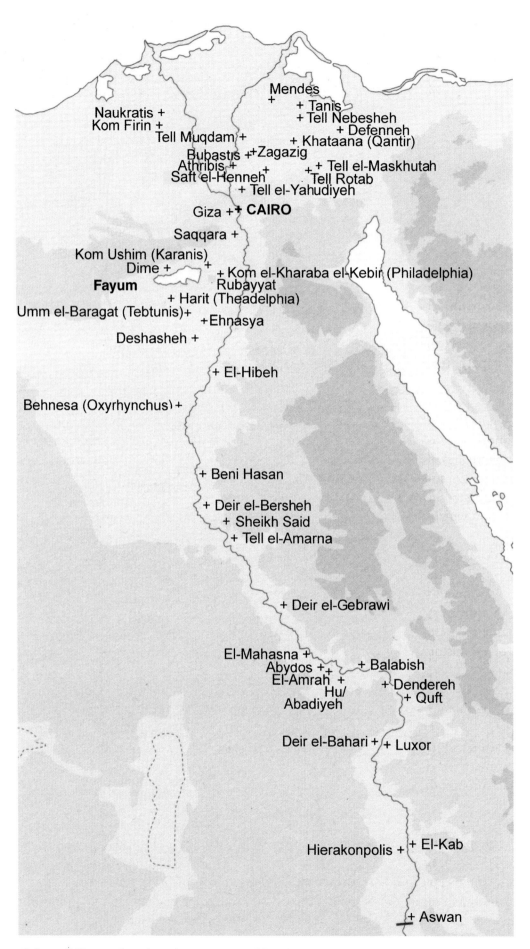

Map of Egypt showing sites excavated by the Egypt Exploration Fund between 1883 and 1915, and other places mentioned in the text.
Map courtesy of Aidan Dodson.

Foreword

When the Egypt Exploration Fund (later Society) was established in 1882, as a result pre-eminently of the labours of Amelia Edwards, it was bringing together in an Egyptian context strands of scholarship which had their origins much earlier in the century. The Napoleonic expedition to Egypt had included in its aims a thorough scientific survey of the country and its antiquities, and the publication of the results as the *Description de l'Égypte*, beginning in 1809, gave the study of Egypt both impetus and a remarkable body of data to fuel research. An even more important result of the expedition was the discovery of the Rosetta Stone which was to lead to the unlocking of the ancient Egyptian scripts and with it the opening up of the pharaonic world as it was seen by the ancient Egyptians themselves. Visits and expeditions to view Egyptian monuments subsequently became commonplace, as did scientific exploration by such notable figures as John Gardner Wilkinson, but the opening up of the country also brought with it an unbridled and quite unprincipled scramble to acquire antiquities for foreign collectors and collections which could not fail to do untold damage to the monuments. It was these ravages which particularly inspired Amelia Edwards to establish an institution which could at least excavate and record the monuments before destruction descended upon them.

In the development of this work there were initially two particularly important drivers. The nineteenth century saw a great increase of interest in establishing the historicity of the Bible, and the involvement of Egypt in the Old Testament record guaranteed that it would be brought into these enquiries. Naville's in the eastern Delta under the auspices of the Fund provides an excellent example of the operation of this factor in Egyptological research. In tandem with the investigation of the historicity of the Scriptures the nineteenth century also saw the awakening of interest in the historicity of early Greek literature, above all through the work of Schliemann at Troy and Mycenae, and the pre-eminence of the Classics in European education ensured that the historicity of the many references to Egyptian sites would come to feature in the Society's work. As an extension of that research the sites of the Graeco-Roman period also became a major part of the programme of the Fund, yielding spectacular results and providing the basis for a publication programme which is still on-going and universally regarded as a model of its kind. However, important though the Classical and Scriptural currents were in orientating the Fund's early research, Amelia Edwards' concern for excavation and recording of monuments asserted itself from the very beginning, and in this context the disinterment of the great mortuary and memorial temple of Hatshepsut at Deir el-Bahari occupies a prominent position. Even at a time when it was possible to employ large numbers of Egyptian workmen for very small sums of money the recovery of the temple and its epigraphic recording must count as extraordinary achievements.

Inevitably subsequent research has moved out from these beginnings, and points of emphasis have sometimes had to change, but the tradition of meticulous excavation and recording established by pioneers such as Petrie, Griffith, Carter, Grenfell and Hunt who feature in this volume set a superb example and will continue to inform the work of the Society in the years to come.

Alan B Lloyd

Naville at Bubastis

and other sites

Neal Spencer

The Egypt Exploration Fund's first fieldwork took place in the Delta and was directed by Edouard Naville, a Swiss scholar born in Geneva in 1844 who had pursued his Egyptological and Biblical interests at universites in Geneva, London, Bonn, Paris and Berlin. Early in his career, Naville's Egyptological research focused on philological matters: copying temple inscriptions, and publishing Book of the Dead papyri. He was also involved in the production of text volumes for the *Denkmäler* of Lepsius.

In 1882, the newly founded Fund appointed Naville as its first excavator. The choice of the Delta was dictated by several factors, most notably the fascination with finding archaeological evidence for Biblical narratives (an interest close to Naville's heart), but also the ability to reach an agreement with the Egyptian Antiquities Service over where to work, and whether there would be a division of finds. The Fund's subscribers were expecting objects in return for their support, and, over 10 years, Naville's work more than satisifed those expectations, as stunning statuary, architecture and reliefs were sent back to adorn the museums of Europe, North America and Australia. Naville's later career was spent in southern Egypt, where he excavated the temples of Deir el-Bahari and the Osireion at Abydos.

Following a reconaissance trip in 1882, covering many of the important sites in the Delta, Naville worked for many years in northern Egypt, at Tell el-Maskhutah, Tell Rotab, Khataana /Qantarah, Bubastis, Tell el-Yahudiyeh, Saft el-Henneh, Mendes and Tell Muqdam. Attempts to work at Khataana/Qantarah (Qantir) in 1885, later spectacularly proved to be the site of Per-Ramesses, were thwarted by high ground water and the lack of harvested fields. In 1891 and 1892, he turned his attentions towards Ehnasya, near the entrance to the Fayum.

The rapid publication of reports on the work at these northern sites was a model followed by the Fund for many years, and these Memoirs are often the only dedicated studies of these sites, which have since suffered considerably. Many of the volumes contain brief descriptions on other sites visited by Naville during the course of a season; some of these have all but disappeared. The title of his first excavation report, on Tell el-Maskhutah, reflects his Biblical interests: *The Store City of Pithom and the Route of the Exodus.*

The photographs from Naville's work reveal a world far removed from modern excavation sites, with hundreds of men employed to clear temples of accumulated debris and to recover statuary, reliefs and decorated architecture. Some provide fascinating glimpses of life on an excavation in the 1880s and 1890s, but the pictures of monuments are often excellent, and frequently the only published image available to Egyptologists.

Naville sought to reconstruct histories of temples through their inscriptions. The photographs underline Naville's interest in the monumental, at the expense of the masses of smaller objects he must have encountered, particularly pottery. In the Delta, this approach can be problematic due to the re-use of stone monuments. Thus at Tell el-Maskhutah, it is now widely recognised that the Ramesside monuments found by Naville were brought from another site. Naville's methods reflected a traditional approach to archaeology, already being superseded by the pioneering Flinders Petrie.

Naville and his colleagues camped by the sites they were excavating; this picture may show their tents by the mounds of Bubastis. The team were obviously without electricity or running water: the large water jar in front of one tent would have been used for washing, cooking and cleaning, and would have been regularly refilled in a nearby canal. Naville was accompanied by his wife Marguerite, Francis Llewellyn Griffith (and from the second season the collector Reverend MacGregor, who took many of the photographs), and the Count Riamo d'Hulst. He would also have hosted visitors and kept a staff of servants. A checklist of items kept in store by the EEF in early 1887 provides a glimpse at the excavators' diet: navy biscuits, gingerbread biscuits, jam, chutney and tins of ox cheek & vegetables, Irish stew, hotch potch, *petit pois* and green pea soup.

Edouard Naville undertook three seasons of excavations in Bubastis, in the eastern Delta, between 1887 and 1889. Here Naville and one of his colleagues, recently identified by Beverley Rogers as the Reverend William MacGregor, pose amongst their workmen for a view of the excavations in progress. The Europeans' clothing make it clear they were directing work rather than being part of it! The depth of archaeological deposits is evident, gradually being dug through and carried away by the basket load. The view is uncluttered by the accessories of modern excavation techniques: gridlines for the trenches, computerised survey equipment, drawing boards and small finds bags and labels. The location of this picture is not evident, but the lack of stone blocks suggests it may have been taken in the sacred cat cemetery to the west of the temple. Naville briefly investigated this badly damaged area, which was much pitted by previous illegal excavations, and found bronze figurines of cats placed in brick-lined pits, at least some of which were also used for human burials. Most of Naville's work at Bubastis took place in the ruins of a large temple dedicated to the goddess Bastet, built during the Twenty Second and Thirtieth Dynasties. The excavations also yielded many statues, reliefs and architecture from the Fourth Dynasty onwards, providing Naville with 'a summary of the history of the country'.

As Naville had to excavate to a considerable depth to uncover the temple ruins, the discovered monuments then had to be lifted out of the resulting pit before they could be transported to Cairo. Here, a wooden pulley is used to lift blocks out; accidents must have been commonplace during the excavations. A letter from the Count d'Hulst back to the EEF describes how while he was 'putting the big jack in position a *fellah* through stupidity dropped it upon my left hand which was reposing on a stone & the result was two fingers broken, two nails of the hand mangled. For three days my arm was swollen up to the shoulder'. The letters from the excavations remain silent about injuries to the workmen, which must have been common. In the centre of the picture lies the monumental sculpture of a sun-disc (see p.18).

The chaotic appearance of the temple remains as Naville removed the layers of debris is very clear here. Two monumental Hathor column capitals, one fallen on its side, the other upright, are visible, with small palm-leaf capitals lying in between. It is likely that the columned hall of Osorkon II featured a central colonnade of Hathoric columns flanked by shorter columns with palm-leaf capitals. Naville could not see these fine sculptures as being the product of Third Intermediate Period craftsmen, and proposed they were usurped Twelfth or Eighteenth Dynasty capitals. However, he recognised how the style of carving was dictated by their intended position atop tall columns: 'Looking at them close by, they seem flat, and destitute of expression; whereas at a distance, the features come out with striking liveliness'.

Many of the large, pink granite blocks found in the eastern part of the temple at Bubastis bore a distinctive series of reliefs. These depicted the royal jubilee (*sed*) festival of King Osorkon II, and remain a fundamental source for study of this festival, which is also attested in reliefs of much earlier periods. Naville understood the reliefs as coming from a gateway. This block includes depictions of divine statues and emblems brought from all over Egypt, but also shows dignitaries prostrate before pharaoh, labelled as 'kissing the ground'. Less than three years after the end of his work at Bubastis, Naville had published reliable line drawings, many the work of his wife Marguerite, of all of the *sed*-festival reliefs, making them available to scholars throughout the world.

Some of the finds were photographed several times, both with and without people. The published excavation report features a similar view of this black granite statue of Ramesses VI, but accompanied by a young, female Egyptian worker. Here, a bearded gentleman wearing an impractical (and surely uncomfortable) outfit favoured by many archaeologists of the time – suit and pith helmet – takes the place of the missing upper part of the statue. His identity is uncertain. Is it Naville himself? Or the Count d'Hulst, responsible for removing blocks from the temple and transporting them to Cairo? Another possibility is Ernest Cramer-Sarasin, Naville's cousin, who was an avid antiquities collector, and who is known to have visited the excavations. Naville deemed this statue unworthy of museum display, so it was left on site.

Two headless scribal statues of the official Amenhotep sit before the ongoing work of digging out blocks from the temple area. Amenhotep lived in the reign of his name-sake, Amenhotep III, and as 'overseer of all the king's works' he must have been closely involved in building activity at Bubastis. The statue on the right, now in the Egyptian Museum in Cairo, features a finely carved scribal kit slung over the shoulder. The other statue was donated to the British Museum. Note the young boy standing to the left of the picture: baskets of rubble and earth were often carried to the spoil heaps by women and young children.

One of the female workers at Bubastis stands beside a wall relief, depicting Osorkon I offering to the principal goddess of the temple, Bastet. As is typical in reliefs from the temple, she is shown as a lioness-headed woman, whereas the vast number of bronze figurines of the goddess found in the nearby cat cemetery show her in the guise of a cat, or a cat-headed woman. This dichotomy reflected her dual nature as both a destructive and a beneficent goddess. Naville seemed somewhat surprised by the quality of these reliefs: 'The good traditions are not yet lost; it may even be said that more care has been taken with those sculptures than with many works of Rameses II, made rapidly and with negligence'.

Naville's excavations revealed statuary and reliefs of several lesser-known pharaohs. This lower part of a seated royal statue is inscribed on the base for 'the son of Re, Khyan, beloved of his *ka*'. Khyan was one of the Hyksos kings, Palestinian rulers who came to control large parts of northern Egypt in the mid-second millennium BC. Statues of this type underline how they presented themselves in purely pharaonic style. The statue was found in front of the gateway into one of the columned halls, and thus must have been re-used in the Third Intermediate Period temple.

A series of colossal column capitals inscribed for Osorkon II were recovered from one of the halls in the late temple. These are carved on two sides with high-relief images of the goddess Bastet, shown with distinctive curled wig and the ears of a cow. The abacus is embellished with a protective frieze of cobras, while the other two sides of the capital bear the king's cartouches. The dualism of Upper and Lower Egypt which pervaded temple architecture is evident here too: the coiled cobra on the side wears the red crown of Lower Egypt, flanking a stylized papyrus stem, the heraldic flower of the north. The capitals from the opposite, southern, side of the hall combined a cobra with white crown and lotus, symbols of Upper Egypt. Capitals of this type were donated to museums in Boston, Sydney, Berlin, Paris, London and Cairo. A column inscribed for Ramesses II lies fallen in the background.

One of the most unusual sculptures unearthed by Naville was this group, in which the gods Horus-the-Child and Amun are seated before a monumental sun-disc. Large sceptres are placed between and to either side of the divine statues. The base is inscribed with the cartouches of Ramesses II and the epithet 'Re of the rulers', but this is a later recarving. This sculpture may well be part of an elaborate sun-disc headdress for a monumental statue, perhaps in the form of a falcon.

The Count d'Hulst was charged with getting the blocks out of the temple and to Cairo, even after Naville had returned to Switzerland. Eventually he brought large iron jacks to move the heavy monuments. The local workmen described these as iron '*afrit*' (demons). The Count then endeavoured to employ donkeys to carry the blocks to the nearest canal, but the workmen wanted a railway and steam engine to be installed. In exasperation, the Count wrote: 'After great efforts in this road-less country, I had managed to bring the locomobile of 20 horsepower … to the Tell, we had the mortification to find that the engine was absolutely unable to move the stones, in fact the stones prevented the engine to move an inch. There remained therefore nothing to us but to move the blocks by men upon wooden rollers. The heat in Egypt is this year quite extraordinary great, the ways have become a very fine grey dust a foot deep & far worse than sand; this makes the work very difficult. It costs great efforts to keep the men at work under this trying heat & it is only by exposing myself to all the hardships with them, that I can retain my power over them'.

Two of Naville's Egyptian *reis*, or foremen, stand by a block bearing an inscription of Ramesses II which invokes the god Seth. Employing hundreds of untrained workmen, Naville would have relied on the foremen to ensure the work went to plan, particularly during periods when he was back in Cairo. Griffith, Naville's assistant at Bubastis was scathing in his later criticisms of the Swiss excavator's methods: 'The work was clearly planned + the plan was frivolously thwarted. The whole business should have been the best piece of work I have ever done but N. knew nothing whatever about excavating; nor how to find things'. The accumulated archaeological deposits which covered much of the temple in the late nineteenth century can be seen in the background.

Using copious amounts of manual labour, ropes, pulleys and ramps, Naville aimed to remove as many decorated blocks from the site as possible. 'I have been much impressed by the fact that the considerable works of sculpture which have been unearthed at Bubastis are doomed to a certain destruction whether by the salt and water or by the hands of the Greeks and the *fellaheen*. Under such circumstances it would be much better to remove as much as possible and to distribute it between the European museums than to let it decay and be ruined'. Over 125 tons of material was removed from Bubastis in three seasons, about a third of which ended up in the Egyptian Museum, Cairo. The standing water just visible in the foreground is a reminder of the often difficult working conditions in the Delta.

The *reis* (foreman) relaxes to the right, while a blur of activity takes place around him. Women and boys are employed to carry baskets of excavated spoil, while the men unearth the blocks and turn them over to check for inscriptions. Naville commented upon difficulties with photography in the field: 'Rev. W. MacGregor and I are amateur photographers; neither of us have made a special study of this delicate and difficult art. For this reason several of the negatives were not very good; besides, whenever some natives are included in the picture, it is hardly possible to persuade them to remain motionless'.

Naville visited Saft el-Henneh, 8km east of Bubastis, in December 1884, and the following spring he sought to find further fragments of a monolithic granodiorite shrine of Nectanebo I. The original discovery of this magnificent monument was related by Naville in one of his letters back to the Fund: 'There, about twenty years ago the *fellaheen* came across a large monolithic shrine in black granite, covered with sculptures and hieroglyphs, and which was at once broken to pieces by command of a *pacha* apparently in order to ascertain whether it contained gold'. Naville's efforts led to the discovery of six further fragments which joined those in the Museum. By the following spring, the partly reconstructed *naos* was on display by the entrance to the Boulaq Museum, as pictured here. It was later transferred to the Egyptian Museum in Cairo when this replaced the Boulaq Museum.

Naville undertook one season of work at Tell el-Yahudiyeh ('the mound of the Jew') north-east of Cairo, with the hope of finding evidence for it being the site of the Jewish settlement found by the High Priest Onias, who fled from persecution in Syria. Disappointed with the lack of monumental remains (this statue of Ramesses II had been excavated prior to Naville's work), he moved into the cemetery area, where late New Kingdom and Roman burials were investigated. The havoc wrought by *sebbakhin*, quarrying archaeological strata to use as fertiliser in the fields, is clear from the mounds and tall open sections visible in the background.

In 1890 and 1891, Naville excavated at Ehnasya (Herakleopolis Magna), 115km south of Cairo. The temple remains he unearthed dated mostly to the reign of Ramesses II, with inscriptions invoking the god Heryshef. Naville had to excavate over 40,000m³ of soil to a depth of nearly 7m to reveal the temple. His spoil heaps rise in the background of this photograph, with the ramps created by the workmen to help them carry out the spoil. This view down into the temple shows part of the colonnade before the façade of the temple proper, with the front of the hypostyle hall behind it. The titulary of Ramesses II is carved into the façade of the building in large scale hieroglyphs, followed by the statement that 'he made (it) as his monument for his father Heryshef, king of the Two Lands'. The rear part of the temple was not systematically investigated by Naville, but in 1904 Flinders Petrie succeeded in recovering most of the ground plan, and discovered reliefs from a Middle Kingdom temple.

The façade of the temple at Ehnasya was fronted with six red granite columns, each over 5m in height, topped with finely carved palm-leaf capitals. The columns are carved with inscriptions giving the names and titles of Ramesses II, accompanied by scenes of the king before the gods Heryshef, Osiris-Naref and Horus. The king's cartouches are repeated upon the abacus. Some of the columns were later recarved with the names of Merenptah. In the foreground lie some of the original column bases; the intact column was later donated to the British Museum.

Two royal statues stand guard by part of the expedition camp at Ehnasya. That on the right fits with a base also found by Naville, inscribed for Ramesses II 'who established monuments in the temple of Heryshef'. The small size of the face in proportion to the torso suggests this is a reworked Middle Kingdom statue, with significant remodelling of the face and the addition of a long beard. The smaller statue has facial features reminiscent of some Ramesside statuary, but it may also be a recut statue of earlier date. In addition to the pharaonic remains, finely carved stone columns and friezes from a late antique building were discovered, some of which lie around the statues in this photograph. Naville was not wholly enamoured of these remains: 'The sculptures representing persons are very coarse work; but some of these flowers and *arabesks* (sic) are very fine, we took them away, and they will make a nice collection of Coptic ornaments'. These may originally have embellished a church built mostly of red brick.

Petrie in the Delta

Patricia Spencer

In Petrie's *Seventy Years in Archaeology* he quotes from a letter he had written to a personal friend on 20 December 1883 when he had just arrived in the Nile Delta; 'I work because I can do what I am doing, better than I can do anything else, in comparison with the way other people do things. I enjoy it because I know that my time produces more result in this way than in any other, and I am aware that such work is what I am best fitted for'. The work which Petrie undertook in the Delta for the newly-formed Egypt Exploration Fund was to establish the foundation of his reputation as the father of scientific archaeology in Egypt.

Petrie's only previous work in Egypt (1881-82) had been to survey the Giza Pyramids plateau and it was the publication of this survey which had so impressed Sir Erasmus Wilson that he prevailed upon the EEF to engage Petrie as an excavator to investigate the site of Tanis – believed to be the biblical city of Zoan. A special fund of £1,000 had been raised to finance the excavation though Petrie himself received no salary for his work, and on 6 November 1883 Petrie left for Egypt. His instructions also included the requirement to travel by boat along the Wadi Tumilat to visit other sites and assess their possibilities for future excavation. With his Cairo friends, Professor and Mrs Amos, he sailed in a *dahabiya* through the Wadi Tumilat to Ismailiya, and then, before beginning work at Tanis, Petrie made an excursion into the western Delta in search of the provenance of a small statuette which he had purchased at Giza. This was eventually to lead him to the discovery of the ancient Greek city of Naukratis.

Petrie excavated for only one season at Tanis, then, with Francis Llewelyn Griffith and Ernest Gardner, moved on to Naukratis, Nebesheh and Defenneh before leaving the Delta in the summer of 1886. His unhappiness with what he saw as 'the constant mismanagement of affairs' then led him to resign as an excavator for the EEF.

The photographs which Petrie took during his Delta seasons were all taken using a home-made pin-hole camera. He developed his glass negatives on site and the images published in this chapter were made from these glass negatives - some of the earliest excavation photographs in the EES archives. Unfortunately Petrie, of whom relatively few photographs exist, does not himself feature on any of his Delta images, but his Delta archive provides a fascinating record of his early work in Egypt and records sites and monuments which have long ceased to exist. Petrie's Delta negatives are divided between the EES Archive and that of the Petrie Museum of Egyptian Archaeology at University College, London with the majority of the 'Naukratis' negatives being stored at UCL.

It is unfortunate that Petrie did not return to the Delta later in his career to rescue the archaeology of other important sites. However, the importance of the work which he undertook in the Delta cannot be underestimated. Tanis today is well-protected and still under excavation by a French mission, while Defenneh, being in a remote location, appears to be just as Petrie left it, but Nebesheh is now totally within, and in places beneath, the modern town of Hosaniya, and Naukratis has been almost totally destroyed.

The current EES Delta Survey owes much to Petrie's inspiration and continues to make the same kind of site-visits as he did. The Survey is published on-line at www.ees.ac.uk and is continually being updated with new information.

A view of Tell Abu Suleiman which was visited by Petrie during his travels (from November 1883) along the Wadi Tumilat before work started at Tanis. Petrie and the Amoses shared the hire of a *dahabiya* called the *Philitis* with a nine-man crew. The ancient town at Tell Abu Suleiman had been founded on a sand *gezira* and had originally covered 6 *feddan*. Another of Petrie's photographs shows a mud-brick wall at the site. During this trip Petrie also investigated a number of other ancient sites: Tell Rotab (where Naville would excavate in 1885), Tell el-Maskhutah (the scene of Naville's excavations in 1883) and the area around the recent (1882) battlefield at Tell el-Kebir. When the *Philitis* needed repairs at Zagazig, Professor and Mrs Amos returned to Cairo by train, leaving Petrie to travel by river when the repairs were completed. He spent these few days visiting Bubastis (another site which Naville would work for the Fund, in 1887-89) and Tell Muqdam, near Mit Ghamr. Petrie himself then had to abandon the *dahabiya* when a closed barrage lowered the water-level, and he too returned to Cairo by train.

As soon as the water-level rose again, Petrie returned to the stranded *Philitis* to travel back to Cairo, and when she became becalmed he took the opportunity to visit the ancient mounds of Athribis (Tell Atrib) near the town of Benha. Today little remains of what was once one of the major *tell*s of the southern Delta but this photograph shows the extent of the mound in the late nineteenth century and the buildings of what Petrie regarded as the 'Roman city'.

At Athribis, in addition to locating a Roman road and columns from Roman buildings, Petrie also excavated and photographed blocks and statues dated to the reign of Ramesses II and to the Twenty Sixth Dynasty, indicating that there must once have been a dynastic temple at the site. This block shows Ramesses II presenting offerings to the god Atum.

Petrie arrived at Tanis on 4 February 1884 and the capricious Delta weather made itself felt from the beginning: 'When I arrived the mounds were almost impassable for the mud, and continual storms threatened my tent'. He had to build a temporary wooden shelter in which he lived for the first rain-drenched week before he could start work on the construction of his house. February was a particularly wet month, though by now Petrie had a corrugated iron roof which kept out the worst of the weather until a torrential downpour in May. Petrie took several photographs of the flooded temple site at Tanis after this ferocious storm and he estimated that about two inches of rain had fallen. In addition to flooding the temple, in some hollows to a depth of six feet, the rain inflicted much damage on his house, washing away the mortar between stones and dissolving brickwork. Then no sooner had the site dried out than the weather became unbearably hot and Petrie closed down the work at Tanis in the middle of June 'after many dust storms, heat over 100°, and violent rain'.

and built this, his first dig-house in Egypt, on top of part of the enclosure wall, beside the entrance to the temple – in the same area now occupied by the house of the present-day French expedition, the small site-museum and the offices and magazines of the Supreme Council for Antiquities. As always, Petrie's accommodation was extremely basic, offering little in the way of comfort. The house, when finished, had several rooms built around a small courtyard and Petrie's graphic description of its simplicity and furnishings (primarily boxes and tins which could be put to many uses) is quoted in Margaret Drower's biography. He also notes how, from the house, he could watch 'how things are going on down in the workings whilst I am up at breakfast' reminding us that, apart from his local workmen, he was alone at Tanis without the assistance of other archaeologists to supervise the work on site. While working at Tanis, Petrie's main source of supplies was the town of Faqus, about 21 miles to the south where could be found basic foods and necessities such as candles and paraffin. Here also, once a week, a trusted boy would collect the cash for paying the workmen, a task which Petrie did himself on site '...this way work is going on while they are being paid, so that they don't sit idle'.

A view taken by Petrie from the door of his house, looking east over the temple site. The jumble of blocks, statues and obelisks are seen as Petrie found them on his arrival in 1884. The only excavation undertaken previously at the site had been by Mariette in 1860-64 and French involvement in excavation at Tanis continues up to the present day. As is the case with many temple sites in the Delta, all the limestone, the main construction stone of the temple itself, had been removed before the modern era, either to be reused or to be burned to make quicklime, leaving behind only monuments such as statues, obelisks, door-elements, etc. which were cut from hard stones unsuitable for reuse. Petrie wrote '..the first day I went over it I saw that the temple site was worked out; the limits of the ruins had been reached, and no more statues or buildings should be hoped for..'. He did, however, examine all sides of as many blocks and statues as possible (either by turning them over or by mining beneath them) to check for evidence of reuse, and he sank a number of trenches outside the main temple area which yielded interesting results.

The excavation of the Roman Period house of a 'lawyer' Aserikhet (called Bakakhuiu in Petrie's *Tanis* volumes) to the east of the temple enclosure at Tanis, gave Petrie a first chance in Egypt to pay attention to the smaller items found in archaeological work which had so often been ignored in favour of colossal statues and monumental buildings. The house had been substantial with upper floors which were not preserved, ground floor rooms and cellars. In it Petrie discovered furniture, papyri, statues, many divine images and items of domestic usage, such as pottery and mortars, as can be seen in this photograph. Virtually all of the objects found by Petrie in Aserikhet's house are now in the British Museum, though the large 'Bes' jar in this photograph was reserved for the Boulaq Museum, the precursor of the Egyptian Museum in Cairo.

Pieces of a stela of Taharqa (above and right). A hand-copy of the stela was published in *Tanis* II with a translation by Griffith. A note in the text points out that 'Mr Petrie's excellent copy was revised by M. Naville from the squeezes'. The lower part of the stela had been known, and copied, before Petrie arrived at Tanis but he was the first to identify the upper part.

This granite block, cut from the great colossus of Ramesses II and reused in the pylon of Sheshonq III of the Twenty Second Dynasty, shows King Sheshonq receiving the sign of life. The block is described in *Tanis* I (p.23) and a very rough line-drawing of it appears in *Tanis* II (pl.IX, No.157). That drawing gives no indication of the fine quality of the workmanship.

In 1883, before making his way to Tanis, Petrie visited Giza where he had worked for the previous two years. He was offered small antiquities for sale and purchased the figure shown in this photograph; part of a small alabaster statuette of a soldier which Petrie recognised as being of archaic Greek or Cypriote work. 'I at once gave the man what he asked for it (never run risks in important cases) and then enquired where he got it. "From Nebireh", was his answer'. Nebireh is in the western Delta, in the region of Damanhur, and Petrie was bound for the eastern Delta to work at Tanis, but the little figure intrigued him and, when delayed in Cairo, he took the opportunity to investigate its provenance further. He took the train as far as he could, then had a 20 mile walk before finally locating the ancient *tell* where he found two of his acquaintances from Giza in search of further antiquities to sell. They showed him the place where the statuette had been found and Petrie noted many sherds of archaic Greek pottery; 'I laded my pockets with scraps of vases and of statuettes and at last tore myself away, longing to solve the mystery of these Greeks in Egypt'. Despite having a high fever, Petrie investigated other sites in the area before returning to Cairo to finalise arrangements for his departure for Tanis.

After a season of work at Tanis, Petrie returned to Nebireh in the western Delta in late 1884 to follow up the lead given him by the alabaster statuette, and, now accompanied by Francis Llewelyn Griffith, lived on the upper floor of a house owned by a local Pasha. It was from the text on this block of stone at the door of the house that Petrie identified the Greek settlement which he had discovered: the stone was part of a decree of the people of Naukratis. This city had been founded in the Twenty Sixth Dynasty and was an important trading-post throughout the Late Period in Egypt. It contained a mud-brick casemate 'fort' almost certainly founded by Psamtek I, and temples in both Greek and Egyptian styles. The excavations also produced much Greek pottery (including stamped amphora handles), weights, coins, scarabs, moulds and many examples of ancient tools. Even in Petrie's day, the ancient *tell* was being destroyed by *sebakh* diggers and looters: 'The area of the middle had been dug out almost to the bottom by *sebakh* workers….this crater of clearance went down about twenty feet under the level of the fields and canal'. Writing in *Seventy Years in Archaeology* Petrie was able to see that 'It was well that we stepped in before all was lost, as now the ground has been filled up with surface stuff and the whole is reduced to cultivation'.

This photograph shows marble architectural fragments from the Temple of Apollo at Naukratis. They were illustrated only as line drawings in *Naukratis* I (pl.XIV). Petrie noted the fine workmanship of the carvings which he thought resembled those of the Erechtheion at Athens. The dedication of the ruined temple to Apollo was confirmed by the discovery of hundreds of bowls dedicated to the god.

One of the Egyptian-style temples at Naukratis produced foundation deposits with plaques of Ptolemy II Philadelphus, model tools, stone vessels and pottery. Petrie describes in *Naukratis* I the discovery of the first deposit: 'The first find, that of the south-west corner, was accidental; some children took refuge from rain in a shaft I had sunk there, and amusing themselves by scraping out the sand of the side of the hole, they found the objects'. Petrie recognised similarities with foundation deposit objects of Hatshupsut in the Louvre and was thus able to predict the locations of a further six deposits, which were excavated more carefully than the first one had been.

This photograph of fragmentary inscriptions from Naukratis was taken on the sill of the balcony of the house in which the excavators lived. The longest inscription was published in *Naukratis* I but only in hand copy. The description of the text says that it is the dedication of a *Palaistra*, probably dated to the fourth century BC but gives no indication of the provenance of the block. The reason for this is made clear in a letter of Petrie's to Reginald Poole (then Honorary Secretary of the EEF) written from the site on 5 April 1885: ' The ΠΑΛΑΙΣΤΡΑ stone is brilliantly clear & legible & I have bought it' (EES Archive XVI.f.25). This serves as a reminder that not all the objects, texts, etc. published in early Excavation Memoirs can be assumed to have been excavated at the sites. Probably the block did come from a monumental building at Naukratis but, since it was purchased, its exact provenance will have to remain uncertain.

This stele from Kom Firin, now in the British Museum, was only published in line drawing in *Naukratis* I. The site of Kom Firin was visited by Petrie while he was working nearby at Naukratis, though he did not himself carry out any fieldwork there. The temple area of the site had already been much disturbed by the time Petrie visited it: 'The greatest depth of the excavations is about forty feet below the top, and the greater part of a third of a mile each way has been removed…some years ago sphinxes were found at the beginning of the avenue, and carried away on carts by a *pasha*'. Nevertheless Petrie felt that 'work there would well repay the labourer'. Kom Firin is currently being excavated by a British Museum expedition.

While excavating at Naukratis Petrie twice made the long journey across the Delta to visit Naville who was then working at Khataana (Qantir) and it must have been on one of these visits that Petrie photographed, *in situ*, the remains of the gate of Amenemhat I. Khataana/Qantir is now recognised as the site of the Ramesside city of Per-Ramesses and is being excavated by a mission from Hildesheim Museum.

In January 1886 Petrie and Griffith, leaving Gardner in charge of the work at Naukratis, started excavation at Tell Nebesheh, which was then on the outskirts of the modern town of Hoseniya. The temple site is now within the modern town and partly overbuilt but in 1886 it consisted of a series of low mounds in a marshy, muddy district 'which could only be reached by wading or swimming in the canals'. The position of the temple area was marked by the remains of this standing monolithic granite shrine which had first attracted Petrie's attention. The shrine is in the smaller of two temples, placed at right angles to each other, and dedicated to the goddess Wadjet. Petrie managed to excavate the temple's foundation deposits, from below the water-table, with the name of King Amasis of the Twenty Sixth Dynasty. At Tell Nebesheh Petrie and Griffith were given a guest-room in the home of a local sheikh, but this was far from palatial, being 'riddled with rats and tunnelled by white ants'. Griffith showed himself here to be a worthy partner for Petrie as he 'kept up an interest in biology, dissecting birds while at dinner, and skinning an ichneumon which hung for several days in his bedroom doorway'.

Digging beneath some limestone chips on the surface of the *tell* Petrie located the foundations of the pylon of the Twenty Sixth Dynasty temple. All the superstructure of this subsidiary temple had been removed, leaving, as at Tanis, only statues, blocks and other monuments made of hard stone. The larger, main temple which originally stood at right angles to that of Amasis, was even less well preserved and Petrie was only able to locate its position when he found a side edge of the large temple foundation-box, typical of temple foundations of the later periods of Egyptian history. By excavating small trenches Petrie was able to trace the full extent of the foundation sand-bed but a search for foundation deposits proved fruitless: they were either too deep to be recovered or had been in the higher levels of the sand and removed by stone-robbers.

This sphinx was found above the remains of the pylon of the Amasis temple at Tell Nebesheh and can also be seen on the photograph opposite. Like many monuments found at Delta temple sites, the sphinx had been much re-used. It was probably originally created in the Twelfth Dynasty but had been reworked for, among others, Seti II and Setnakht. Other statues and blocks found in the temple site bore the names of Senwosret III, Ramesses II (a colossal statue almost seven feet high now in the Boston Museum), Merenptah and Ramesses III, indicating that there had once been a much earlier temple at Nebesheh, though any trace of it has probably been destroyed by the cutting of the later main temple foundation located by Petrie.

The ancient cemetery at Tell Nebesheh dated from the Ramesside Period to the Thirtieth Dynasty with subterranean tombs, mostly not well-preserved, but with many points of interest. Some of the tombs had pottery coffins of a type since well-attested at other Delta sites while others showed evidence of foreign influence (in the New Kingdom) from the Near East. However, the most impressive tombs were those of the Twenty Sixth Dynasty, a time when there appears to have been extensive refurbishment of the temple complex. This photograph shows, as found, the basalt anthropoid sarcophagus of an official named Psamtek whose family held important offices in the town of Imet. This, and other texts found by Petrie and Griffith at Tell Nebesheh, confirmed the ancient name of the site. The Psamtek sarcophagus lid is now in the British Museum.

Petrie first saw the site of Defenneh from the top of Tell Ginn several miles away while on one of his walking excursions from Tanis. In 1886 he left Griffith in charge of the excavation at Nebesheh and, with 40 men, boys and girls, walked the fifteen or so miles to Defenneh which was then remote and difficult of access. There were no villages nearby so Petrie and his workforce, which eventually grew to around 70, had to camp on the site. The tent on this photograph (the negative of which is not well preserved) is Petrie's own. 'There is not another soul within ten miles of us, nothing but the sand, and tamarisk, and marsh and water, and desolation. But I like it better than the more civilised places; one lives with the people more, and the ever fresh air and living in a tent doubles one's peace of mind and contentment at once'. Petrie also appreciated the fact that his remote encampment was well beyond the reach of any of the local authorities, especially any officials or *sheikh*s who might expect him to socialise.

The main structure excavated by Petrie at Defenneh is the casemate 'fort' built by Psamtek I, foundation deposits of whom Petrie found under each of the building's corners. It is usually identified with the fort of 'Daphnae at Pelusium' noted by Herodotus. Having already excavated a casemate 'fort' at Naukratis, Petrie immediately recognised the constructional similarities with the Defenneh structure. Another similarity with Naukratis was the large number of imported Greek ceramics associated with the complex, though those at Defenneh were earlier in date. The site also yielded jar seals with the names of Twenty Sixth Dynasty kings, over 1,400 weights (now in the British Museum) and much jewellery, leading Petrie to suggest that Defenneh was the region's centre for jewellery production.

Photographed in front of one of the plastered walls of the 'fort' at Defenneh, the *reis* (foreman) Mohammed el-Gabri was one of Petrie's most trusted workmen. His father, Ali Gabri, had originally been a basket-boy on Vyse's Giza excavations in 1937 and had accompanied Petrie while he carried out his first fieldwork in Egypt, surveying the Giza pyramids between 1881 and 1882. Mohammed would also seem to have worked for Petrie from the Giza days as in 1889 Petrie said Mohammed had been in his employ for eight years. Mohammed, with one of his brothers, worked as a *reis* for the inexperienced Gardner during the second season at Naukratis, and Mohammed then worked with Griffith at Nebesheh until he accompanied Petrie to Defenneh. After Petrie left the Delta, he continued to employ Mohammed on his work in Upper Egypt until 1889 when Petrie dismissed him after discovering, at Hawara, that Mohammed had been taking from workmen between a quarter and a third of any *bakhshish* they had been paid. Petrie was sorry to lose Mohammed's services as he was an intelligent man and Petrie had previously always found him to be trustworthy, but he felt that 'the work could not be allowed to suffer by his greed'. Petrie never again employed a *reis* on his work in Egypt, preferring to deal directly with the workmen himself.

The Archaeological Survey

Christopher Naunton

The Archaeological Survey of Egypt was conceived as a second branch of the Egypt Exploration Fund's activities, to be conducted alongside its excavation work. The reasons for its establishment were explained in a report presented to the Fund's Annual General Meeting in February 1891 by Frances Llewelyn Griffith, who conceived the Survey and was appointed its first Superintendent:

> 'It is not difficult for one who has studied Egyptian archaeology in the country for some years to see what is required in order that the archaeological inheritance of so many centuries may not be swept away at the very moment when the world appears ready to receive and appreciate it. What can be done to stem the torrent of absolute destruction? Here and there a single tomb or temple can be put under lock and key by the action of the Government, or some learned society may undertake its restoration. But history, science and art demand more than this. The Nile valley contains a multitude of monuments and ruins, some partly described, some as yet almost unknown, but all alike exposed to the attacks of the dealer in antiquities, the quarryman and the wanton iconoclast'.

The aim of the Survey was thus to preserve the salient features of Egypt's standing monuments – 'the harvest that hastens to ruin with every day that passes' – through careful recording of the architecture, reliefs and inscriptions.

When making his initial proposal to a previous AGM in November 1889, Griffith had envisaged a 'rapid sketch-survey' which 'might in a few years sweep the whole surface of the country'. However, preliminary work suggested that the scope of the project might need to be revised and Percy Newberry, whom Griffith had appointed to direct the work in the field, recommended the Survey begin by selecting a single site which could then be thoroughly studied. The Fund thus chose to begin work at Beni Hasan, in Middle Egypt, site of the Middle Kingdom local governors of the sixteenth Upper Egyptian nome, and their officials. During the first season (1890-91), Newberry was accompanied by George W Fraser, a surveyor, and Marcus W Blackden, an artist, who was to assist Newberry with the copying of the decoration in the tombs and to produce colour facsimiles of the most important details. Over the course of the next two seasons the team was joined by Newberry's brother John, as surveyor, and two more artists, Percy Buckman, and the seventeen year old Howard Carter, on his first assignment in Egypt. The coloured drawings were intended to capture the finer details of the decoration inside the tombs. They reflect the ancient Egyptians' artistry and also the observational skills of the Fund's artists, each of whom interpreted what they saw in their own way. The drawings were exhibited in London and Manchester during 1893, and they, along with the photographs presented here, derive from the first three seasons during which work was undertaken at Beni Hasan and three other cemetery sites: Deir el-Bersheh, Sheikh Said and Deir el-Gebrawi. The Survey was suspended thereafter for several years due to a lack of resources and the pressing need to complete the publication of the work already undertaken. It would resume in 1898-9 under the direction of Norman de Garis Davies, initially at Saqqara.

Although the aim of producing a comprehensive survey record of the country's standing monuments as Griffith had originally conceived it has long since been abandoned, the motivations behind his idea remain relevant, and epigraphic work and the survey of standing monuments remain an important component part of the Society's field work to this day.

Many rock-cut tombs in Egypt commonly saw further human activity of one kind or another after the burial of the individuals whose memory they were intended to perpetuate. Although they were intended for the mortal remains and associated funerary equipment of the deceased, tombs were often subsequently pressed into service as dwelling places for hermits, travellers and, centuries later, archaeologists and Egyptologists. Newberry appropriated tomb no. 15 at Beni Hasan for exactly this purpose, though whether he would have agreed with Griffith that tombs in Egypt provided 'pleasant… lodgings for explorers' is perhaps open to question.

GEBEL 'EL GEBRÂWI.

SHEIKH SAID.

As a means of setting the scene - visually - for the work to be described in the published volumes, Percy Buckman painted views of each of the areas in which the team worked. Three were published, in black and white, those of Sheikh Said (above), Beni Hasan (the southern tombs, opposite below) and Deir el-Gebrawi (opposite above). A fourth, unpublished example is preserved in the Society's archives (see p.93). It is signed by Buckman and almost certainly depicts the area of the city of Tell el-Amarna, looking south from the northern group of tombs.

The recording of minute decorative details required the use of a little special-
ist equipment, as described by Fraser in the season's report for 1890-91: 'On ar-
riving with Mr. Newberry at Beni Hasan (November 25th, 1890), my first work
was to construct a scaffolding consisting of two trestles and some ladders. The
ladders were used by us continually all the time we were at work, and one of
the trestles was afterwards adapted and used by Mr. Blackden while painting'.
Griffith had calculated the total area of the decorated surfaces to be recorded at Beni
Hasan and issued the following invitation in his report on the 1889-90 season to the
Fund's AGM, should anyone have been in any doubt as to the size of the task ahead
of the team: 'Let him who would realise what this means mount a ladder and trace a
fresco in one of our ancient churches. He will then appreciate the steady devotion of
the copyist to his task of twelve thousand square feet'.

Although the Survey's brief was to record standing monuments, a certain amount of 'clearance' was sometimes necessary, and in some cases tomb shafts were excavated, revealing hitherto unknown chambers. This unlabelled and unpublished photograph shows the clearance of a shaft, possibly that of the tomb of Baket (tomb no. 15) at Beni Hasan, which Fraser described as follows: 'A gang of men who had been started on a large well (shaft)...soon got into stones; and this proved very troublesome. It was 80 ft. deep, and we lifted not less than forty tonnes of stone out of it. With the able assistance of Mr. Blackden, however, a tackle was constructed which drew up a hoist made up of an old box...'. The rocks had been deposited there in antiquity presumably by the plunderers who had removed any substantial objects from the chambers at the bottom and had then gone to very considerable lengths in bringing such a mass of stone in from the hillside.

The Fund's surveyors and others often explored the cliffs and *wadi*s behind sites such as Beni Hasan, in the hope of finding previously unrecorded sites and monuments. On Christmas Eve, 1891, Newberry and Carter set off on just such an expedition, and came across the alabaster quarry of Hatnub, which until then had been known only by name, from ancient textual records. By this point, a rift had developed between Carter and Newberry on one side and Fraser and Blackden on the other. The latter pair, keen to make a name for themselves, visited the quarries a few days later to copy the inscriptions, with a view to publishing them quickly after their return to England, so as to claim the discovery as their own. This led to Newberry's resignation from the Fund, and to Carter gaining his first archaeological experience as Flinders Petrie's apprentice at Tell el-Amarna, in place of Blackden, who now found himself out of favour. Newberry re-joined the team the following season, but Blackden and Fraser did not.

This scene comes from Beni Hasan tomb no. 3 of Khnumhotep II and shows the tomb owner spearing fish. It is reproduced here in a black and white line drawing as the scenes were published in most of the Survey's reports. The drawing accurately reflects the layout and distribution of the various textual and pictorial elements of the scene, but clearly does not capture the finer details. However, this is itself a reflection of the lengths to which the Egyptian artists went to convey accurately the activity in question. In terms of the scene's overall significance many individual elements – birds, fish or other animals – play only small roles, and yet each is rendered uniquely, in fine detail. Drawings of this kind were inked in London using the pencil tracings made in the field, often by artists who had never even seen the originals. The technique was adequate for purely philological purposes, but as Carter himself wrote 'from the point of view of Egyptian art, the results were less than satisfactory'. The texts are little more than extended captions describing the scene in which Khnumhotep, described as being 'great in fish, rich in wild fowl, loving the goddess of the chase', is shown catching fish in a papyrus marsh.

This bush filled with different species of birds of was painted by Blackden in 1891. It comes from the same wall of the tomb of Khnumhotep as the fishing scene and is itself only part of a larger scene of the tomb owner catching birds in a net. A variety of species is shown, each rendered in great detail by the Egyptian artists and captured skilfully by the Fund's copyist. The drawing was published as the frontispiece to the fourth volume of the *Beni Hasan* series. At the top left is a part of the rope used by Khnumhotep to close his net, and the line across the bottom represents the top of the doorway leading to the shrine, which housed a statue of the deceased. A second bush at the other side of the net contains further species of bird which were reproduced individually by Carter.

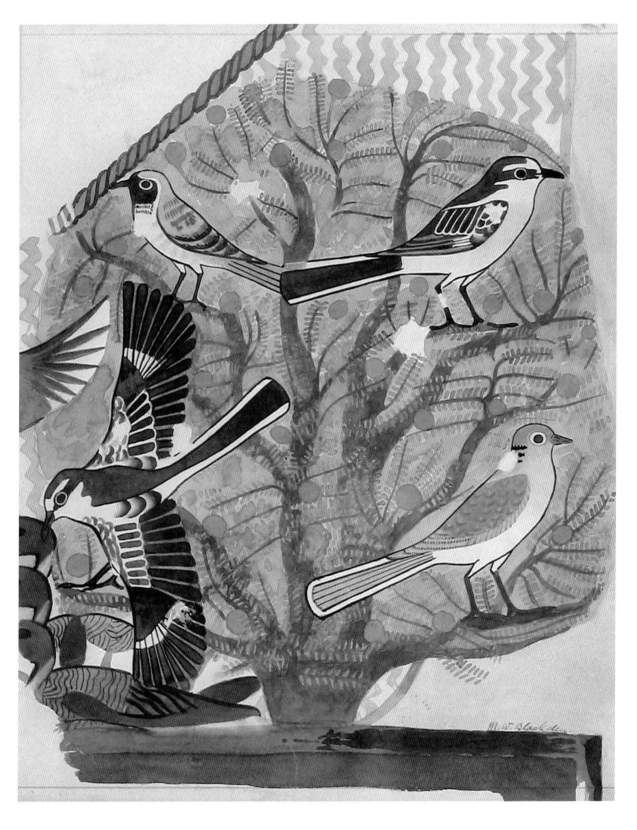

Carter was most interested in making 'careful coloured drawings of the more interesting and important details among these mural decorations'. This cat is part of the fishing scene on p.77 (above and to the left of the two fish speared by Khnumhotep) and is shown balancing on the stem of a papyrus plant which is bending underneath its weight. Griffith was inclined to think that it is in fact a domestic cat, and may even have belonged to the tomb owner, despite its apparent independence: '...it must be remembered that the domestic cat is very apt to stray and hunt for itself'.

The hoopoe shown here, was painted by Carter, and comes from the bush on the other side of the net, in the scene of Khnumhotep catching birds. The difference in the respective styles, and indeed intentions of the Survey's artists is evident in the contrast between the bird shown here and those in the image on p.79. It is also interesting to note that this was acknowledged at the time by Newberry, who felt that the original paintings themselves had decayed to the extent that the artists should be allowed a certain license to 'interpret' what remained: 'Mr. Blackden aimed at ascertaining the original design in a somewhat diagrammatic style: Mr. Carter and Mr. Brown copy faithfully what they see, and render it in its present condition'.

'The goddess of the marshes', from the tomb of Khnumhotep II, was painted by Carter in 1895. Many of the details reproduced for the published volumes were painted by Carter and Percy Brown in 1895, after the Survey had been put on hold. At this point Carter was still working for the EEF at Deir el-Bahari as chief epigrapher to the excavation directed by Edouard Naville at the temple of Hatshepsut (see the following chapter). The image here shows a single hieroglyph of a woman holding a captured wild bird of some kind in her right hand. In this context it represents the name of the goddess Sekhet who dwellt in the marshes and protected those who worked there. The sign is part of an inscription above the scene of Khnumhotep spearing fish, and gives his name and titles/epithets, one of which is 'beloved' of Sekhet. Note that Carter has also added his distinctive initials to this drawing.

The third volume in the *Beni Hasan* series is devoted to the reproduction in colour of individual details from scenes published in full in earlier volumes. The level of detail with which individual elements of often very large scenes were rendered, meant that much had to be left out of the black and white copies. Newberry recognised that there was much in this detail that could help to clarify the meaning of certain scenes or texts. This unusual depiction of a man holding hands with a baboon, from Beni Hasan tomb no. 14, of Khnumhotep I, is in fact a 'determinative' hieroglyph - a sign which has no phonetic value but which helps to clarify the precise meaning of the foregoing signs, which in this case were read as 'Anmutef' (now usually read as 'Iunmutef') a priestly title.

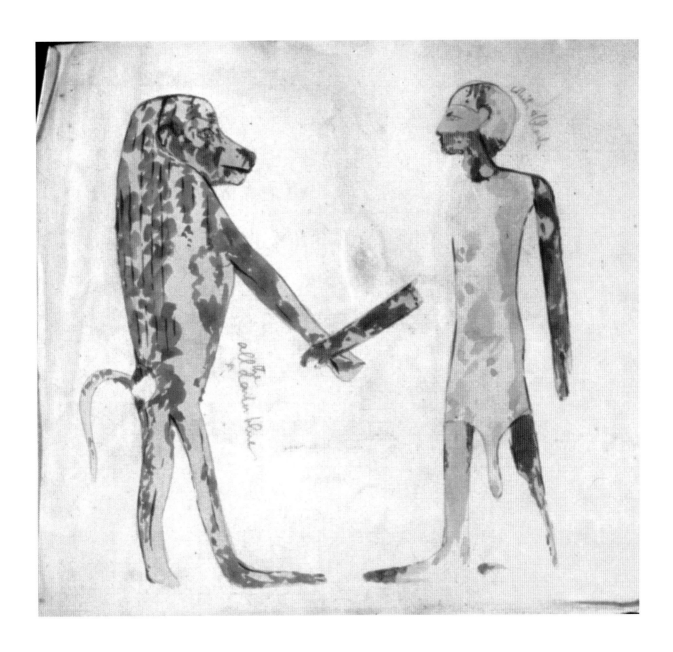

Hieroglyphic signs could be used to convey either the sense of words or their abstract phonetic components, and in their simplest form were rendered simply in outline, or in cursive 'shorthand' forms, with little visual similarity to the pictorial originals. Here, however, it is noticeable that the artists who designed and painted these signs invested in them the same level of detail as they would purely pictorial representations of the same animals. Such is the level of detail involved that, out of context, what are in fact glyphs could easily be mistaken for pictorial illustrations with no semantic meaning, and signs such as this, reproduced by Carter, are indistinguishable from those employed as elements of pictorial scenes elsewhere in the tombs. The curious ram-goat hybrid here, represents the god Khnum, and is complemented by a jug, which in this context has the same phonetic value as the name of the god. It forms part of the name of the tomb owner Khnumhotep, meaning 'Khnum is satisfied'.

This 'setep' sign, from Beni Hasan tomb no. 2, of Amenemhat, was painted by Blackden in 1891 and is a good example of how the internal detail provides more information as to the object depicted by the sign. The colours used clearly show the separate copper or flint blade of the adze, bound to the handle with 'a strong lashing'. Beneath the blade a block of wood is shown to have been hollowed out by the blade. This has little bearing on the meaning of the sign in this context however: it forms part of the word '*setepu*' meaning 'choice things' – food etc. to be made as an offering to the tomb owner, in this case the local governor, Amenemhat.

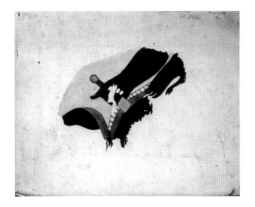

During 1891 Blackden copied several details in tomb 2 which related to the production and use of flint knives. These were augmented by copies made in 1895, after the Survey had officially finished work, by Carter and Percy Brown who was assisting Carter at Deir el-Bahari. Here Blackden has painted only the detail showing a butcher or cook's hand using a flint knife to cut an incision in the neck of an ox. Unlike some of the other details published in *Beni Hasan* III, Newberry felt these were not executed with any great finesse but included them nonetheless as the subject matter was so unusual.

This facsimile shows a scene of the treading in of seed by a flock of sheep from the tomb of Djehutihotep at Deir el-Bersheh. By the time it was recorded by the Survey, the wall had been badly damaged, perhaps partly as the result of an earthquake, and indeed Carter painted this part of it as an isolated fragment suggesting it was not affixed to the wall at this point. Carter's copy was perhaps not made on behalf of the Fund, in fact, and may instead have been one of many details he painted for sale to tourists. His signature has been added at the bottom left hand corner.

This photograph in the EES Archive was taken in the tomb of Djehutihotep at Deir el-Bersheh in 1889, the year before the Survey started work at the site. It shows the famous scene of a colossal statue of the tomb owner, tethered by ropes to a sled on which it is being dragged along by four gangs of forty-two men. The photograph was taken by a Major Brown, who worked for the Department of Irrigation. The scene is of great importance for the information it provides on the transport of large sculptures, while the importance of the photograph lies in the fact that shortly after it was taken the scene was vandalised and almost entirely destroyed, to the extent that Newberry and his team found only a few small parts still remaining on the wall.

This watercolour is signed by Buckman and almost certainly depicts the area of the city of Tell el-Amarna, looking south from the northern group of tombs. The Survey had begun work on the tombs of Akhenaten's courtiers at Amarna in February 1893 without having secured the necessary permission to work at the site. After a matter of a few days, but not before the team had 'measured and planned several of the tombs, copied many of the inscriptions and reproduced in colour some of the fresco paintings', a message was received from the head of the *Service des Antiquités*, Jaques de Morgan, denying the team the permission it needed, and the work was abandoned. As a result Buckman's painting was never published.

PERCY BUCKMAN.

Deir el-Bahari

T G H James

Amelia Edwards had little to say of Deir el-Bahari in the account of her 1873-74 visit to Egypt: 'The Temple of Dayr el Bahari .... would probably be, if less ruined, the most interesting temple on the western side of the river'. She later wrote more fully and enthusiastically about Hatshepsut and her temple; she would undoubtedly have put her weight behind the proposal that the Fund should work at Deir el-Bahari, and would surely have been proud of the results achieved. Sadly she died in 1892, one year before Edouard Naville opened his campaign which would finally reveal the extraordinary monument which has now become such a tourist attraction.

Naville's appointment to work for the Egypt Exploration Fund at Deir el-Bahari was bitterly opposed by Flinders Petrie, who saw Naville as no excavator but a clearer of monuments, but for Deir el-Bahari this was perhaps appropriate as in 1892 the area of Hatshepsut's temple resembled an industrial wasteland covered with the detritus of subsequent occupations, including the substantial remains of a Coptic monastery. Furthermore, scree from the cliffs on the western side continually added to the overburden on the temple area.

Naville began his clearance in the Spring of 1893 and the task was essentially completed in the winter of 1894-5. His principal architectural adviser was Somers Clarke, a distinguished church architect who had developed a special interest in the conservation of ancient Egyptian buildings. Naville's most important assistant was Howard Carter, only nineteen in 1893, engaged to draw the temple reliefs, but from the start used as a general factotum. After clearance the work of consolidation, reconstruction and drawing continued until 1899.

From an early point in his work on the Hatshepsut temple, Naville had thought it proper that the Fund should extend its operations to the area to the south, which he identified as an Eleventh Dynasty necropolis. Funds, however, were not available until 1903. Then Naville resumed work with, as his co-director, Henry R H Hall of the British Museum, who was much more of an objects-man than his colleague.

It soon became apparent that the area was occupied by a far more important monument than had been expected, namely, the funerary complex of King Nephepetre Mentuhotep of the Eleventh Dynasty. A central feature, surrounded by a pillared ambulatory, was identified by Naville as a podium on which a pyramid had stood. It is now considered more probably to be a representation of the primeval mound. Between the western side of the ambulatory were six chapels and tombs of royal ladies. Naville and Hall found four of these burials, one of which contained the finely decorated sarcophagus of Kauit, now in the Egyptian Museum in Cairo. An unexpected find in the Eleventh Dynasty temple was a group of statues of the Twelfth Dynasty king, Senwosret III, who had established a cult there in honour of Nebhepetre Mentuhotep. One of the most spectacular of the discoveries made in the course of this excavation was that of the Hathor shrine which properly belonged to a temple of Thutmose III of the Eighteenth Dynasty, the main part of which was only discovered in the 1960s. The fine limestone reliefs of the temple had been comprehensively vandalized or otherwise damaged over the millennia, and there was no possibility of reconstruction as had been undertaken in Hatshepsut's Temple. There was, however, some compensation in the discovery of many fine sculptures and a wealth of small antiquities. The Fund's work at Deir el-Bahari was concluded in early 1907 and although several other expeditions have since made major discoveries at the site, it is to the lasting credit of Naville and the Egypt Exploration Fund that the possibilities of the site were first appreciated, and the major structures revealed.

General view of the Deir el-Bahari temple area taken in the early days of the clearance. The huge quantities of debris obscuring most of the site are very visible on the right; as also the runs of scree from the cliffs which contributed largely to the overlay. The tower of the Coptic monastery and the gateway of Thutmose III on the Upper Level of Hatshepsut's temple stand above the mostly buried colonnades of the Middle Court. To the left lies the as-yet unidentified temple of Nebhepetre Mentuhotep. This photograph and many others included in this chapter were taken by Howard Carter who became the official photographer of the Hatshepsut excavation, as well as organiser of the recording of the decorations of the temple.

Howard Carter is here seen supervising a group of workmen moving material cleared from the temple site in one of the Decauville cars which Naville borrowed from the *Service des Antiquités* along with 460 metres of tramway. By using this railway it was possible to move great quantities of rubble with relative ease well away from the ancient site. Although engaged to oversee the copying of the scenes and inscriptions of the temple, Carter was also employed by Naville in many other tasks, including the supervision of the clearance and the reconstruction of the damaged parts of the temple. Through these extra activities Carter was able to acquire valuable experience in the managing of an excavation during the many absences of Naville who had teaching obligations in Geneva.

The Upper Court of the Hatshepsut temple before the removal of the considerable ruins of the Coptic monastery, the 'Monastery of the North' (in Arabic *el-Deir el-Bahri*) which gave its name to the area. The Christian buildings were removed wholesale in the clearance of this Upper Court or Level. Naville's lack of interest in these Coptic remains was not uncommon for his time (and indeed for many later excavators) but there was some justification for their dismantling and removal in that many inscribed fragments from the more ancient temple had been incorporated in the monastic buildings. The standing gateway which formed the entrance to the Upper Court is inscribed for Thutmose III, who instituted considerable work on the temple after the death or removal of his royal aunt/stepmother. Many of her representations were defaced.

Naville (on the right) observes the extraction of a substantial architrave belonging to the north side of the colonnade of the Middle Court. At the time of clearance very little of the original structure of the Hatshepsut temple remained intact, much of the masonry having been vandalized and dismantled in late antiquity. A major task of the Egypt Exploration Fund was to reconstruct as much of the temple as possible - work undertaken principally by Howard Carter. Somers Clarke, who generally supervised the reconstruction, reported in 1898: 'I cannot speak too highly of Mr Carter and the resources he has shewn in bringing the work towards a new conclusion without any accident ....'.

Among the many unusual scenes in Hatshepsut's temple are those in the northern half of the Colonnade in the Middle Court devoted to the divine birth of the queen, resulting from the 'marriage' between the god Amun and Ahmose, wife of Thutmose I. This sequence of scenes was designed to legitimize the royal status of Hatshepsut whose proper authority otherwise only lay in her regency while Thutmose III, her nephew and stepson, was a minor. It was a 'device' used occasionally later when it seemed necessary to reinforce the claim of a monarch to the throne. The scenes in the so-called *mammisi*, or 'birth-house' in Late Period and Roman temples render the sequence a common and necessary ritual demonstration of divine legitimacy for the king depicted. In the relief shown here Queen Ahmose, clearly pregnant, is led to the birth chamber by the ram-headed god, Khnum, and the frog-headed goddess, Heqet. The 'flares' on the figure of the queen are the result of damage to the original nitrate negative.

A watercolour of the head of Queen Ahmose, from the relief in the north sequence. It is one of several paintings made by Howard Carter while he was working at Deir el-Bahari. His sensitive reproduction is far more than a straightforward copy. The original is in the London Offices of the Egypt Exploration Society, but Carter subsequently made a number of further copies which he gave to friends or sold to visitors to Thebes.

This painting, the largest of Howard Carter's facsimile watercolours of scenes in Hatshepsut's temple, shows a relief in the innermost room of the small Anubis chapel opening off the Altar Court on the north side of the upper Court. King Thutmose I and his mother Queen Senseneb are shown making offerings to the god Anubis whose figure is no longer preserved. Hatshepsut showed particular veneration for her father Thutmose I and his wife Ahmose. It was from her parents that she derived her royalty, to justify her usurpation of the Egyptian monarchy from her nephew/stepson Thutmose III. Carter's copy, now in the Society's Offices, reproduces accurately the vibrant colours which survive on many parts of the temple's reliefs.

The original drawing by Howard Carter of a scene in the inner sanctuary of the Hathor shrine. The goddess as the divine cow suckles the queen who kneels beneath her. The cow is led by Amun, and to the left Hatshepsut and Thutmose III are shown offering milk and wine respectively, to the goddess. Carter made his drawings in soft pencil at a scale of half life-size, not by tracing, but by drawing free-hand. He and his fellow artists became especially skilled in making out texts which had been deliberately defaced. The original drawings for the whole temple are now in the Griffith Institute in Oxford.

The chapel on the north end of the colonnade of the Middle Court is specifically dedicated to the mortuary god Anubis, along with associated necropolis deities. The structure of the chapel was virtually complete on clearance, and its reliefs and inscriptions retain most of their paint. The figure of Hatshepsut has in all cases been defaced. The scene shown here is undamaged, depicting Thutmose III making an offering of two bowls of wine to falcon-headed Sokar, the god of the Memphite necropolis.

A general view of the Deir el-Bahari site with, in the foreground, the so-called lower shoot, where the Decauville cars were brought to be emptied into a depression where stone had been quarried The choice of this spot for the dumping of debris from the clearance was determined by its distance from the temple area and the apparent lack of ancient remains in the quarry. Some years later, the Metropolitan Museum of Art's excavators recleared the quarry and found the concealed tomb of Senenmut, steward of Hatshepsut, to whom is credited the creation of the queen's unusual mortuary temple. Many fragmentary sculptures of Hatshepsut were also found. In the centre of the photograph Naville's excavation house can be seen.

The clearance of the Middle Court of Hatshepsut's temple. The mounds of debris beneath the Upper Court covered the colonnades which contained some of the most important sequences of scenes and inscriptions in the temple: to the south side of the central ramp (on the left) the sequence commemorating the expedition to Punt, and beyond it, the shrine of the goddess Hathor; to the north (on the right), the upper sequence depicts the coronation of Hatshepsut as King, crowned by her father Thutmose I, and the lower sequence records the marriage of Ahmose and Amun, and the divine birth of Hatshepsut. Further to the north is the beautifully decorated shrine of Anubis.

After the clearance of Hatshepsut's temple, Naville was determined to extend the Fund's work to the south; he therefore undertook a clearance of part of the deposits overlying what he thought was an Eleventh Dynasty necropolis. Here work is shown in progress with the boundary wall of the Hatshepsut temple on the right, leading back to the Hathor shrine. The huge piles of debris fairly indicate the expected magnitude of the clearance. In fact the rubble concealed the presence of a substantial monument, the main structure of the mortuary temple of Nebhepetre Mentuhotep. One of Naville's practical concerns was to be able to undertake this extension of the work while he still had the loan of the Decauville cars and tramway from the *Service des Antiquités*.

On the north side of the Upper Court is a series of rooms, including chapels devoted to various deities, among whom are Amun and Anubis. An open court in the centre of the suite of rooms contains a huge altar dedicated by Hatshepsut to Re-Horakhty, the solar deity who combined the natures of the quintessential sun-god Re and of Horus 'of the horizon'. The setting of this altar, open to the sky and the sun, significantly suggests the *plein-air* character of the worship of the Aten as practised at Tell el-Amarna in the reign of Akhenaten, a century later, when the Aten was identified with Re-Horakhty.

A view of the Eleventh Dynasty temple taken from the heights of the cliffs forming the bay containing the funerary monuments of Nebhepetre and Hatshepsut. What can be seen principally is the main structure of the temple, the central podium set in a pillared hall, with colonnades on three sides at a lower level. The tombs of the royal ladies on the north side of this central complex lie along the side closest to the viewer, on the right. Naville postulated the existence of a pyramid on the podium, basing his interpretation on a mention in the Abbott Papyrus of the Twentieth Dynasty, which contains the report on the inspection of tombs in the Theban necropolis. The king's tomb is there called a pyramid. Careful investigations by German archaeologists in the 1960s concluded that on structural grounds there could not have been a pyramid, but possibly a form of the primeval mound. 'Pyramid' in the Abbott Papyrus is probably used loosely for a royal burial structure.

A passage, approximately 150 metres long, descends from the centre of the peristyle court to the west of the podium, deep into the cliffs. For the greater part of its length it is lined with sandstone slabs, shown in this photograph. It terminates in a granite-lined chamber which seems undoubtedly to have been intended, if not actually used, for the royal burial. No trace of the burial was found but there was a mass of fragmentary wooden models, statuettes, weapons and boats.

The limestone sarcophagus of Kauit was found in the tomb of the princess, one of the four found by Naville and Hall on the west side of the central podium. It is made up of individual slabs, one of which, a side slab, is shown here. The decoration on this sarcophagus is stiff and very formal, but technically very well executed. In the centre Kauit is shown seated on a high-backed chair, her hair being dressed by a female attendant. In one hand Kauit holds a mirror, and in the other a shallow bowl from which she drinks. A male attendant in front pours drink from a bowl, saying: 'For your *ka*, lady. Drink what I give you'. The drink is probably milk, for to the left are shown two cows with calves, one being milked. The reassembled sarcophagus is in the Egyptian Museum in Cairo.

At the far west end of the hypostyle hall, the innermost section of Nebhepetre's temple, there was a small shrine, with an altar hall where some fine, brightly painted relief blocks were found. In this photograph the prominent block, still *in situ* shows the upper part of a figure of the king wearing the white crown. He is making offering to an unidentified deity before him; behind him is a figure of Hathor, badly defaced. This block, now in the Metropolitan Museum of Art, New York, is one of the few surviving substantial fragments of the remarkable decoration in this temple, which marked the revival of fine relief work after the First Intermediate Period, when the Old Kingdom tradition of highest quality sculpture and relief carving was temporarily lost.

King Senwosret III of the Twelfth Dynasty established a cult in the Deir el-Bahari temple in honour of Nebhepetre Mentuhotep, who was revered as the monarch who reunified Upper and Lower Egypt after the troubled time of the First Intermediate Period. Six life-size granite statues of Senwosret were erected on the upper colonnade surrounding the main structure of the temple, but all had been tumbled and damaged some time later in antiquity. Four, lacking their feet, but otherwise relatively intact, were found in the course of the excavation, and are here shown in the court of Naville's excavation house. They are considered to be fine examples of Middle Kingdom royal sculpture, and one in particular shows the king in a masterly manner, often considered, probably inappropriately, as depicting him worn down by the cares of government, a sad, tired, ruler. It, along with two others, is in the British Museum and the fourth in the Egyptian Museum, Cairo.

In 1906 Naville's expedition uncovered a remarkable, barrel-vaulted shrine on the north side of Nebhepetre's temple and close to the western cliffs. It was intact, with fine reliefs, and contained a splendid life-size figure of the Hathor cow. The scenes in the shrine concern King Thutmose III, and it is now known that the shrine formed part of a small temple of that king built above those of Nebhepetre and Hatshepsut, the greater part of which was not discovered until the 1960s. The fine figure of Hathor as a cow incorporates a royal figure in front, and another in relief at the side, kneeling and being suckled by the goddess. The name of Amenhotep II on the cow's neck indicates that the figure was made or completed in his reign; he is surely the subject of the two royal representations. The shrine and cow are now in the Egyptian Museum, Cairo.

A general view of the bay of Deir el-Bahari after the completion of the Egypt Exploration Fund's work. Following the final campaign in December 1906, Naville wrote: 'there will be no more at Deir el Bahari since we may now say that Deir el Bahari is finished'. To make such a claim is nearly always a mistake. From 1911 to 1931 the Egyptian Expedition of the Metropolitan Museum of Art worked at Deir el-Bahari and in the valley leading from the east, and found many important ancient structures and objects. In particular, the quarry in the left foreground of this view, which had been used by Naville as his principal dump, was cleared out; many broken sculptures of Hatshepsut were recovered and the 'secret' tomb of Senenmut, steward of the queen and 'architect' of her temple, was discovered. In the 1960s the Polish Centre of Mediterranean Archaeology, working with the Egyptian Antiquities Organisation, uncovered the Thutmose III temple in the area to the south and above the Hatshepsut temple, here covered by scree. Naville's dig-house lies in front of the Nebhepetre temple, in the left-centre of the view here.

Abydos

Barry Kemp

Abydos in the nineteenth century AD still preserved much of an ancient ritual landscape. The cult of Osiris, the ruler of the kingdom of the dead, became rooted here towards the end of the Old Kingdom and remained so until the very end of ancient Egyptian culture. It left traces of two thousand years of devotion, superimposed upon an earlier millennium of more local history. It was served by a town built around a group of small temples, by an extensive cemetery and by a field of greater and lesser monuments spread across several square kilometres of desert.

The chief monument was the temple of Seti I, cleaned of its sand in 1863 to expose its painted and exquisitely carved reliefs, and immediately a must-see on the traveller's itinerary. At the same time the large sanded-up cemeteries were indiscriminately attacked for their portable antiquities whilst the ancient town was methodically quarried for its soil, to be spread on the fields as cheap fertilizer. It was a common enough pattern of rapid destruction, brought on by an appetite for collecting antiquities and by agricultural modernization, pursued at a time when few appreciated the importance of archaeological context.

The Egypt Exploration Fund's initial four seasons of excavation (1899/1900–03) exemplified a broad change of perception and practice that established archaeology as a serious scientific method of study, not only in Egypt but throughout much of the world. The distant past began to take the shape that we now take for granted. At Abydos, in a brusquely efficient way, the Fund was highly successful in this new field, both in the range of information recorded and published, and in the richness of material discovered.

Much of the credit rests with Flinders Petrie who, aged 46 and with twenty years of fieldwork in Egypt behind him, commenced a re-clearance of the tombs of the kings of the First Dynasty in November 1899. Two seasons later, the work completed, he transferred to the town site and the scant wreckage of its cluster of temples for the cult of Osiris, and struggled to bring order to a complex many-layered site that had lain for centuries buried in damp soil. All the time that he toiled, a group of archaeological assistants directed excavations in other parts of the huge ruin field, especially the site of Abydos South, 3.5 km distant from Petrie's base in the ancient town. Here lay a series of royal monuments, including a model town, that are still far from being understood, although their underground architecture perhaps reproduced the Egyptian idea of what the realm of Osiris looked like.

With hindsight one can now regret that no one saw – or had the resources to do anything about it if they did – the underlying unity of the Abydos ruins. The place was instead worked as a series of sites largely isolated from one another, a situation that still persists today, a hundred years on. None the less, the six volumes of excavation reports with their distinctive red-lettered black spines, remain a fundamental source of information for anyone who wants to reconstruct the elusive antique landscape of piety and ritual that was Abydos.

The tombs of the early dynastic kings at Abydos were built in pits cut into the desert. They consisted of a chamber for the burial and many, many more to store the king's burial furniture. The king in question here was Khasekhemui, last of the Second Dynasty and thus only a short time before Djoser, builder of the Step Pyramid at Saqqara. All the chambers were originally roofed with wood. Once the burial was made, sand was heaped over the top, perhaps kept from blowing away by a long-vanished retaining wall. Flinders Petrie, cloth-capped and standing on the left, a measuring staff in his hand, watches his workmen dig out the sand from some of the storerooms. The remnant of the sand mound looms in the background, precariously held back by a rough stone wall that the workmen have built along the very edge of the pit. Health and safety at work legislation is easily mocked, but a picture like this makes you realise why we have it.

Behind this statue lies an inspiring story. As told by Petrie, his workmen present him with a tiny ivory statue that bears the name of Khufu, builder of the Great Pyramid. It is the first (and it remains the only) statue of this pharaoh to be discovered, ever. It measures just over 7 cm from the base to the top of the crown. The trouble is, it is headless. Petrie gets some of his men to spend three weeks sifting through the spoil heaps and, miraculously, they find the tiny, tiny head. It is a story for optimists (or for cynics, if you think the workmen were teasing Petrie). The statuette is now in the Egyptian Museum, Cairo.

Something the looters left behind. A human arm, wrapped in linen, that had gone to the grave wearing armlets of gold, turquoise, lapis lazuli and amethyst. It was found in the tomb of King Djer of the First Dynasty, and might have been his. As we see it in the photograph it represents a choice in how we want to view the past. Display it just as it was found, and we have a richly informative context around which discussions develop but in which the jewellery is not shown at its best. Extract the jewellery, exhibit it as art, and it becomes as soulless as the merchandise in a duty-free catalogue. The choice is actually theoretical. As far as we know, the arm no longer exists. The jewellery is, however, on display in the Egyptian Museum in Cairo.

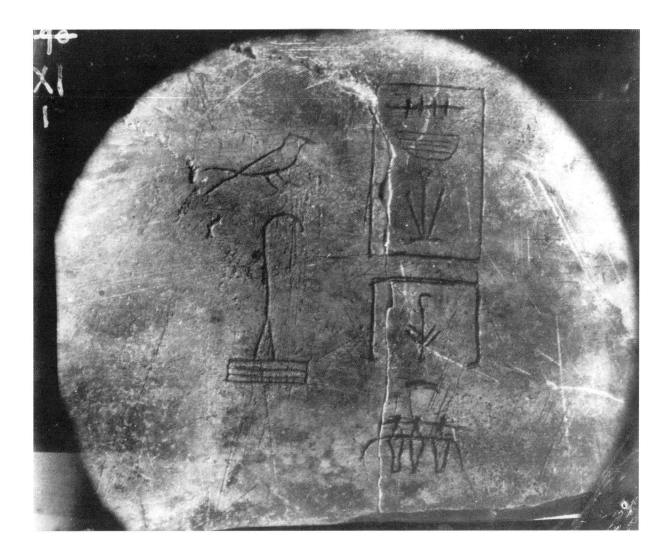

By the time Petrie began, the early royal tombs had already been thoroughly turned over. The sheer quantity of loose sand and building rubble ensured, however, that many ancient objects still remained undetected. One attractive category comprised broken pieces of bowls and other vessels made from stone, in the kind of quantities that matched the pottery of other periods. Sometimes they bore short hieroglyphic texts, as here. Scratched into the side of a grey diorite bowl from the tomb of king Qaa is a short vertical text that seems to give the name of a building or administrative division. The circular framing of the photograph comes from the use of a close-up lens.

Technology from a hundred years ago. Usually it brings a smile of condescension at things that are beautifully engineered, ingeniously contrived but definitely quaint. Not so in archaeology. We use the latest in electronic survey equipment because we are borrowing from a commercially buoyant sector. But equipment that has no use outside archaeology is of no interest to commercial manufacturers. The archaeology market is too small and poverty-stricken. So, on looking at Petrie's ingenious rig for drawing sherds, one makes a mental note to have one built for one's own use. Technological progress, nil.

Because they were beneath the ground in an area where sand naturally accumulated the early royal tombs were remarkably well preserved. These walls, of sun-dried mud brick, are still standing at least 2.5 metres high, despite being roughly five thousand years old, of the reign of Peribsen, another late Second Dynasty king. The picture also gives an idea of the volume of loose sand that had to be carried out to free them. Petrie was, in one way, lucky. Another archaeologist, Émile Amélineau, had already, and only a short time before, cleared most of it out. He had intended to return to carry on his work but was hindered by 'unforeseen circumstances' back home in France. The first he knew that Petrie had usurped him was when he read about it in a newspaper. But we all agree that Petrie did a better job.

Unskilled labour has always been unreasonably cheap in the Egyptian countryside. It encouraged archaeologists to think big and work fast. Here, at Abydos South, is the site of a monumental mud-brick layout of the time of King Senwosret III of the Twelfth Dynasty, put there probably to create a tomb that would never be used except, in the imagination, by the king's spirit seeking the presence of the god Osiris. The site measured about 150 metres by 250 metres, was buried in loose dry sand, and was the target of an excavation intended to last for only a single season of a few months. All that could be done was to follow walls and keep an eye open for stray finds. In the excavation report a clear plan of the building appears. But the greater part of the site, the white spaces between the walls, remained unexcavated.

Symbol or a way of saving on building costs? Beside Senwosret III's spirit tomb at Abydos South were large, brick subsidiary tombs (whether real or symbolic has never been satisfactorily established). The edge of one of them is on the right side of the picture. As at the king's own building (and visible in the last photograph), one of the walls, whilst thin, follows a serpentine course. Such walls are well designed to withstand lateral pressure and so to hold back encroaching sand. But with ancient cultures the prosaic often does not seem to be enough. We look for (or invent) added layers of meaning. Serpentine walls occur at several Middle Kingdom royal tombs. Are they, like an enveloping serpent, tail in mouth, protecting the tomb or symbolising its eternal endurance?

The way into Senwosret III's dummy tomb at Abydos South was by a vertical shaft and a separate sloping descent passage (visible at the top of the photograph). The shaft, 20 metres deep, is here being emptied of its sand. The workmen are lifting out the sand fill, basket by basket. To do this they are utilising the ancient lining of the shaft, made from unmortared mud bricks that in one place are wedged with little pieces of stone. The steps are original. The tomb contained an empty sarcophagus and fragments of stone vessels, suggesting that a mock burial had been put in place.

Egyptian temples were buildings to house acts of devotion to the spirits that dwelt in statues. The most important were statues of gods, and at Abydos the most important of the gods was Osiris. But statues of kings and of honoured individuals were also donated and received the same treatment. Over time Egyptian temples must have come to resemble museums of sculpture. Here, amidst the debris of ancient demolition, lies the head of a red granite statue, made to a scale larger than life, that was probably attached to a square back pillar. The severe features, now exaggerated by the bruising of the stone, are probably those of King Senwosret III of the Twelfth Dynasty. It is now in the British Museum.

'Those who built tombs, their places are gone. What has become of them?… Their walls have crumbled, their places are gone, as though they had never been' (a song from the tomb of King Intef). We will never know what the terraced temple of King Ahmose I at Abydos South really looked like. The toiling men are uncovering only the massive retaining walls to the terraces that ran up the mountainside and on which the temple had been built. 'Of the great stone temple nothing was left but the hundreds of tons of chippings' wrote the archaeologist in charge. It has indeed gone as if it had never been. And having been freed of the protecting sand by archaeologists, the newly exposed terrace foundations will begin an inexorable progress towards the same fate.

What did one do with all those tons of stone chippings and sand? Limited resources meant that the only solution was to heap them up in dumps closely beside the excavation and then to leave them there permanently. There is always a danger that such dumps will actually cover unexcavated features of interest. On the other hand, in this location they might come to protect the site, as they slump back down again, and even act as a wind-break against the driving sand-laden winds that will eat at exposed mud-brick walls. The photograph, a northwards view along the lower terrace of Ahmose's temple, captures the scale of the Abydos site. Petrie's base camp lay along the line where desert met fields, more or less above the left-hand figure in the line of workmen.

Later temples were frequently built at the expense of earlier ones. The older stonework was taken down and the blocks then re-used. Here a list of offerings from a temple built under the Eleventh Dynasty King Nebhepetre Mentuhotep (his prenomen cartouche is present at the left end of the block) has become part of the foundations of a later temple. On it stand the wooden tripod legs that supported Petrie's surveying instrument, which he used to take large numbers of levels – tops of walls, surfaces of pavements, positions of individual objects. This was a valuable step in recording the site in three dimensions.

Behind the town of Abydos lay extensive cemeteries for the people who lived there and perhaps for others who came from further away to benefit from being buried close to the tomb of Osiris. In use for more than three thousand years, the cemeteries preserved a record of changing burial customs for the whole span of ancient Egyptian culture. Here the top of a pottery coffin lid, made for a child, records how, in the later centuries, a cult of the god Bes also became established at Abydos. Bes, a dwarf with lion features, protected people from the outside world through noise and aggressive postures. A suitable patron for archaeologists perhaps.

One of the most important improvements in excavation method has been the recognition that it is better to remove the layers of material that fill an ancient site by working from the top evenly across a defined but open area. In this way a record can be kept of the layers of the fill itself, and one has a better chance of recording the positions of objects found in relation to how the site – often it will have been a building – was laid out. The older style of work, at least in Egypt, was to have a line of workmen advance along a moving front, removing all the fill at once, as if quarrying. In this view of a town built to accompany Senwosret III's ritual layout, the excavated rooms are on the right, the unexcavated ground on the left. The mound in the distance marks the site of a pyramid of King Ahmose I, part of his ritual layout, and perhaps the last royal pyramid to be built in Egypt.

Layers of history. The limestone blocks are the foundations for a temple to Osiris built by King Amasis (Ahmose II) of the Twenty Sixth Dynasty, inside the huge temple enclosure at the original town site of Abydos. It was bigger and sturdier than its predecessors, and to make way for it the existing ground was levelled over a broad area. This must have sliced off many archaeological layers, because the new, flat lower surface of the ground was soil that filled the spaces between the walls of buildings that dated fifteen hundred years earlier. These walls belonged to a combined town and complex of little shrines of the late Old Kingdom. It is these, built not of stone but of mud brick, that Petrie's workmen are digging out, perhaps riskily in view of how close they are to undermining the heavy stone blocks.

In the ruins of one of the later stone temples at Abydos Petrie found the smashed remains of 'four figures in hard white limestone, two seated, and two standing joined together'. Attracted by the 'masterly rendering of the face', he commented that 'it has a full vitality and realism in the expression which might well have been copied from the best type of the modern Egyptian peasant girl'. He added that 'the whole of the pieces are now in the Cairo Museum, and, when the figures are restored, a full publication of them on a large scale, will be essential'. That has not happened just yet: many intended archaeological publications take more than a century to complete. On the seated statue is the cartouche of King Nectanebo II of the Thirtieth Dynasty. Art historians are sure, however, that the standing female statue (the one shown here) was made during the Middle Kingdom.

The more ambitious rebuilding of the temple to Osiris was accompanied by setting a new limit to the temple enclosure. It was made larger and defined by a massive wall of mud bricks constructed, in the manner of the times, in a series of separately made sections of different thicknesses and with curving bedding planes for the bricks. In the part shown here (known as Kom es-Sultan) it ran across a corner of the ancient town mound that had probably been abandoned centuries before. The new wall sections were laid in huge and deep foundation trenches, their depth probably marked by the step in their lower parts. In the years before Petrie's arrival the villagers dug out a good part of the ancient town, so lowering the ground level inside the enclosure and exposing the foundations of the great wall. What is left of this much earlier material – layers of soil, rubble and sherds filling spaces between the thin walls of houses – belongs to the Old Kingdom. It is an important relic of the first town of Abydos. Petrie did not stay long enough to give it any attention other than the taking of this photograph.

For the first time in perhaps thirty-three centuries, the steward of Memphis, Amen-hotep, faces the camera. He lived in the latter part of the Eighteenth Dynasty. His way of being represented for eternity in the temple of Osiris was to leave a statue of himself there, perhaps arranged whilst on a pilgrimage to Abydos. In the hieroglyphic inscription he asks to share in the various ceremonies performed in the temple, affirming the righteousness of the life he has led.

El-Amrah, el-Mahasna, Hu and Abadiyeh

Joanne Rowland

Fieldwork in Egypt at the turn of the nineteenth/twentieth centuries was quite varied in terms of the quality of both excavation and recording. At the forefront of archaeological methodology stood Flinders Petrie, a household name to amateur and professional Egyptologists and archaeologists alike. Petrie, working with his wife, Hilda, his students and his colleagues, was responsible for the excavation and publication of a number of Pre- and Early Dynastic cemeteries, including those covered in this chapter: el-Amrah, el-Mahasna, Hu and Abadiyeh.

El-Amrah and el-Mahasna are areas within the greater Abydos cemetery while the cemeteries of Hu and Abadiyeh were published by Petrie in *Diospolis Parva*. This chapter publishes for the first time photographs of, and information about, the 1909 work in Cemetery F at el-Mahasna: the unpublished field records are in the Society's Archive.

It is thanks to work conducted on material from early cemeteries, Hu and Abadiyeh in particular, that the relative chronological dating of early Egyptian artefacts, and henceforth tombs, became possible. Jacques de Morgan, working in Abydos, was the first to realise that the large number of burials which Petrie had considered to post-date the Old Kingdom were in fact, prehistoric. However, it was Petrie's methods of seriation and sequence dating which allowed, for the first time, for ceramic vessels, stone vessels and other small finds to be placed in chronological order. His work has provided the basis for chronological refinements that have been made ever since and for the implementation of seriation for statistical analysis in many disciplines. Scientific volumes on the study of Pre- and Early Dynastic Egypt are now, thankfully, on the increase, and the interested student is encouraged to seek out the works of Adams and Ciałowicz (*Predynastic Egypt*), Hoffman (*Egypt Before the Pharaohs*) and Midant-Reynes (*The Prehistory of Egypt*) as sound starting points.

This chapter is intended to engage with the method and practice of archaeology in Pre- and Early Dynastic cemeteries during the late nineteenth and early twentieth centuries, and will hopefully give some colour to the scholars who conducted these excavations, as well as allowing a number of previously unpublished photographs to be seen: photographs which have largely not featured in the site publications of the day, but which are valuable and insightful for excavation methodologies of the time. The names which appear on the following pages are those of Arthur Mace (Flinders Petrie's cousin and student), David Randall-MacIver, Anthony Wilkin, Edward Ayrton and W. L. S. Loat. It seems appropriate here to make a note about the lesser-known Mr Anthony Wilkin. Wilkin, although mentioned in autobiographies and biographies of Petrie, is not credited with authorship of the 1902 volume of *El-Amrah and Abydos* having died of dysentery in Cairo before the fieldwork was completed. Wilkin was already a trained artist when he arrived in Egypt and he became an able assistant on Petrie's excavations. He also travelled with Randall-MacIver to Libya. The resulting volume, *Libyan Notes*, was published in 1901. He is fondly referred to, posthumously, in the 1901 volume *Head-hunters* by Alfred Haddon as 'my pupil, friend and colleague …. Barely twenty-four years of age, and with the promise of a brilliant career before him'. References to Wilkin through Haddon's book also confirm his photographic competence and his interests in sociology and natural science.

This chapter is dedicated to the memory and sadly brief career of Mr Anthony Wilkin.

The Petries record passing by the site of el-Amrah in late 1899. The site was then in Amélineau's concession for the Abydos region in Upper Egypt and they note that it had been 'recently turned over'. David Randall-MacIver with Anthony Wilkin, and later Arthur Mace, excavated the early cemetery at el-Amrah between 1899-1901, employing workmen from the town of Quft in Upper Egypt, numbering nearly 40. These archaeological foremen are known as 'Quftis' and are still employed widely in Egypt today by foreign missions, as are the 'Qurnawis' from Qurna. Petrie noted that 'well-trained men' needed little direction and that 'their observations and knowledge should always be listened to'. He also believed, as he says in *Ten Years Digging in Egypt*, that it was important that workmen think about subsurface remains, for the reason that they might better proceed with caution, and avoid damage to the archaeology.

Fieldwork accommodation can vary enormously depending upon location, and some early excavators, notably Flinders Petrie himself, sought accommodation in tombs. In the early 1880s, Petrie was very fond of his 'home' at Giza, noting that 'often when in draughty houses, or chilly tents, I have wished myself back in my tomb'. His 'home' at Giza, he explains, was actually a three-roomed abode, consisting of offering chambers rather than a proper tomb. Although Petrie is often noted as one who did not indulge in home comforts, his reasoning behind his choice of accommodation was rather more practical; to keep cool in the heat and warm when the weather turned cold. Randall-MacIver and Wilkin, however, constructed their own dig house in close proximity to the excavations. The construction, with straw on the roofs and mud-brick for the walls, as used then and now in local villages, is very suitable for the climate. Their compound comprised their living quarters, together with a sizeable courtyard in which to store, record and study the artefacts found.

This wide open space in front of the dig house at el-Amrah allowed for the various types of ceramic objects to be studied and grouped. In the foreground, ceramic coffins and jar burials are laid out, with the fourth jar from the left still containing the remains of the deceased. The coffins shown here are of similar types to those found in the Pre- and Early Dynastic periods throughout Egypt. That all of these ceramic vessels have been laid out according to their type is indicative of the fact that the excavators were students of Petrie. Ceramics were not universally accepted as items of great value by scholars of early Egypt at the end of the nineteenth century and the on-site destruction of ceramic vessels, and other finds, was not unheard of. Petrie, however, knew and emphasised the importance of ceramics and small finds, and stressed the need, on pain of dismissal, not to mix finds from different contexts.

Ceramic coffins of various types and shapes were used from the Predynastic period right through until the Roman period. The individual in this coffin had been placed in the flexed position, typical for all types of graves, from simple pit burials to mud-brick chambered graves, of the Pre- and Early Dynastic period. While it was often only graves of greater interest (frequently those which contained grave goods) that were published during this era, at least one of each variety of burial type per cemetery usually received some attention. No grave goods can be detected within the actual coffin in this burial and this was the case for the majority of non-elite burials in the Pre- and Early Dynastic periods. From its close proximity within the pit, only a single pot appears to be associated with the interment. Sadly, because there is no 'north' arrow in the picture, it is not possible to comment on the orientation of the individual and whether they are positioned in a common manner, or otherwise.

Whoever buried this individual must have considered the deceased to have been of some importance or wealth. This coffin is placed within what is called a chambered grave, that being a grave with one or more additional areas for storage of grave provisions, and the photograph shows that there were pots both next to the coffin and in the adjoining chamber. These coffins are one of the ways in which the deceased was protected from the ground. This form of protection may well be a development of the earlier and contemporary burial practice of laying the deceased on, or between, sheets of matting and/or animal skins, which is noted even in the early pit burials at Merimde Beni Salama.

A scene that would not be out of place today, the workman stands barefoot with his *faz/touriah* (a type of hoe) resting on his shoulder, excavating what is described as a typical Predynastic tomb. In Petrie's time, as often still today, ownerships of one's tools (hoe and basket) was a prerequisite of gaining employment as a member of the workforce. Other more specialised tools were, and are, supplied, and Petrie notes that items of occasional need would be found by 'the master'. However, the individual was expected to maintain his own equipment. Additional tools recommended by Petrie for excavation were crowbars (which he notes can be obtained in any Egyptian town), ropes, large hammers, cold-chisels, stone-saws, saw files, fine wire sieves as well as native sieves, which, Petrie notes, were also locally available.

Petrie arrived at Abadiyeh on 29 November 1898 together with his team, which included Mace and Randall-MacIver. He noted how the region was covered with a number of cemeteries 'all of a good period for learning archaeology' and Petrie was in fact looking for additional prehistoric data to aid him in his task of ascertaining the relative dates of various artefacts. It was not uncommon to find these types of artefact in early burials. With the exception of the broken flint knife, the objects shown are made of copper: an axe head, an adze and what appears to be a chisel. Petrie published an example by which to date copper and bronze adzes in his 1904 publication *Methods and Aims in Archaeology* and noted that the age could be 'told at a glance'. The presence of these kinds of objects within a tomb could be an indication of the occupation of the deceased, or in some instances (where broken flint knives and broken copper adzes are found, for example) be related to some form of pre-burial ritual. The objects are displayed at an angle, hence the pins inserted beneath them and they are in remarkably good condition, probably due to their deposition in the dry desert sands – similar copper artefacts, if excavated in the wetter climes of the Nile Delta, would certainly have exhibited greater signs of corrosion.

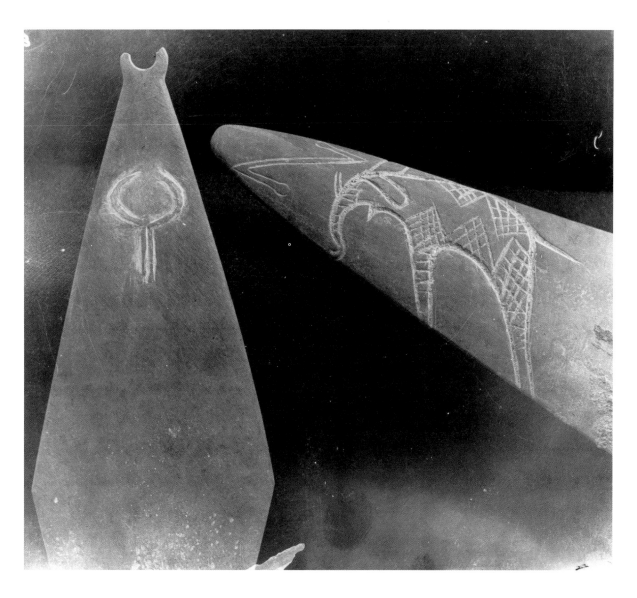

The original publication of these objects only allowed for the view from one side, that being the photograph showing the elephant motif. It is interesting to consider why the reverse side (also decorated) was never included in the original publication. They can be seen here together for the first time. This practice was not, however, unusual, since many palettes – including decorated Early Dynastic examples – have often been either published or displayed so as to show only one side. These 'cosmetic palettes' were fairly frequently placed in early graves; their original purpose was as a surface for grinding pigments for cosmetic purposes.

From the disturbed nature of the bones in the middle of the grave, it would seem highly likely that this tomb had been subjected to robbery at some point in either the Predynastic period, or later during the Dynastic period. Many tombs, especially larger tombs, were robbed in antiquity. However, the fact that, despite the robbery, so many ceramic vessels remain in this larger than average tomb, confirms that a high status, or well respected, individual had been buried. It is useful to have these photographs of burials with the vessels still *in situ* since it shows that even at this early date, those burying the dead had thought about placing different kinds and sizes of objects in different parts of the tomb, something which Petrie made record of in his notebooks. It is only a shame that, once again, we do not have a north arrow in the picture, which might help us to visualise where the body might have originally lain.

Allowing for a view into the distance at Diospolis Parva, this arrangement of artefacts dates to Petrie's Gerzean phase, which falls within the Naqada II phase in modern revisions of dating. The clues as to the period within Petrie's chronology, famously published in *Disopolis Parva* in 1901, are the handles on the vessels on the top left, the fish shaped palette in the centre and the dark on light decoration of the large pot in the centre. Looking closely, it is possible to see a register of large and small flamingos running around the bottom of the largest pot – such motifs are very common on ceramic vessels of this phase.

Archaeological photography, today, is both a science and an art, with efforts to obscure the devices used to hold the artefacts in position, having to be made either in the field or digitally, at a later date. However, Petrie was a master of the camera, extremely knowledgeable about its mechanical functions and the use of various models and types of lenses in various circumstances. In the previous photograph, as here, ingenuity and availability are the keys to the arrangement of a series of stone items found in tomb 152 in the cemetery of Hu. The three strangely shaped objects on the left hand side of the picture are called 'mace heads'. Numbers 151 and 300 are earlier disc types, but number 198, the pear-shaped variety became and remained a part of royal icongraphy; later depictions of the striding pharaoh wielding his mace are commonly found on temple walls throughout Egypt.

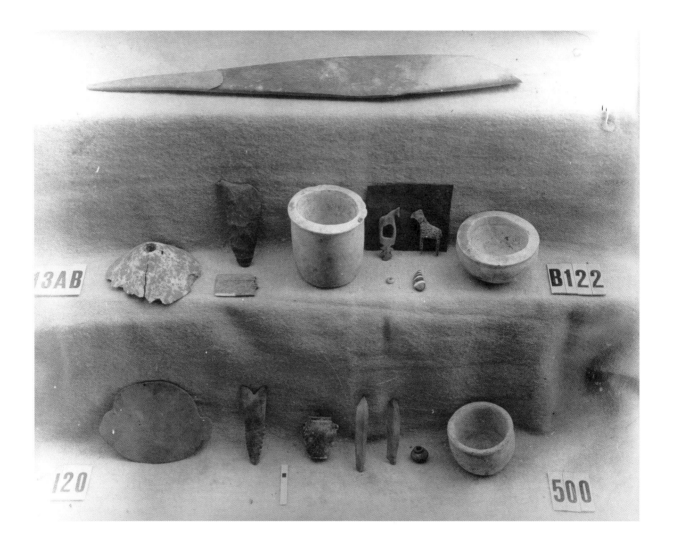

The wide variety of objects that could be found in Pre- and Early Dynastic graves are well represented here and include not only the beautiful fish-tailed flint knives (bottom, second from left), but also more common flint blades and beautifully carved animal flints, as in the middle row. The arrangement of these objects on steps is purely a practical issue. The cameras of this date were bulky and not easily manoeuvrable and Petrie advocated using a vertical position for photography of portable objects, since this enabled an oblique light to illuminate the objects. Modern cameras are much lighter and smaller, and sophisticated tripods make it simple for the photographer to position the camera directly above the objects so that they may be arranged horizontally on the ground, or on a table.

11 ABADIYEH   GRAVE B 107

An interesting combination of early Predynastic (Petrie's Amratian period, partially contemporary with the Naqada I and II phases) objects. The stones on the upper ledge of this previously unpublished photograph would appear to be rough hand axes, and the larger stone could be a mace head, although without any indication of the possibility of a hole for attachment, it is more likely a stone pounder. The pottery at least is very typical of the Amratian phase, with this white 'cross-lined' decoration on a dark red polished surface. It is just about possible to make out the depiction of a crocodile, or possibly a lizard, on the oval-shaped dish on the bottom level. Both geometric and naturalistic elements featured as decorative elements on Naqada I vessels.

Excavations began at el-Mahasna at the beginning of 1909, after Edward Ayrton and William Loat, while they were working at Abydos, had been made aware of the robbing of cemeteries at nearby el-Mahasna. The excavators noted how they set up camp with 'five tents …. a cook, three dogs, and twenty-five workmen'. The workmen can be seen up on the sand dune and are largely carrying out a process of sand-clearance of what were very shallow pit graves. Cemetery F, until now, remains unpublished and the photographs published here cannot all be assigned exact provenance, nor as we shall see, can the tombs shown here be ascribed exact dates. This may prove to be a similar case to Cemetery E, which is referred to as 'The Mixed Cemetery'. The photographs have been examined alongside descriptions on the tomb cards and chapters from the publications on Abydos. There is a note which states that the tomb cards are 'Ayrton's Cards' from Abydos 1908-9. These cards are noted to have been 'worked up by Loat in conjunction with negatives from Abydos 1909. Cemetery F'. This first view from a distance shows the workers up on the raised ground, a little away from the cultivation, where burials were commonly placed in antiquity. Burial on high ground kept the dead away from the rising flood waters and away from the cultivable land, which starts just to the right of the picture. The figure in white may well represent the Qufti foreman of the local workforce.

At first glance it would seem that this plate illustrates the excavation of a large Pre- or Early Dynastic tomb of mud-brick - the photograph is labelled 'Abydos. Cem F. Tomb 4. Natives at work'. While the small Cemetery F tombs discussed so far are more commonplace, larger tombs of the period are known from the sites of Hierakonpolis, Naqada and Abydos. However, the tomb card for Tomb 4 confirms that this is unlikely to have been a large Predynastic tomb as the finds included 'blue glaze ushabtis', indicating a date no earlier than the New Kingdom. The other finds, amongst them an alabaster vase with a lid and half of a grey stone vase, could feasibly have been early finds, however, and it is possible that the tomb had been reused. Despite these dating problems, the photograph is enlightening regarding methods of excavation in the early twentieth century and shows practices that are unlikely to be seen today, with few of the health and safety considerations of today's archaeologists in place. The ladder poking up from the tomb would have been the sole access for local workers to the tomb, the walls of which would seem not to have been shored up. In the foreground it is heartening to see the sieving equipment, two stacked circular sieves, stacked, because the re-excavation of many sites, including Abydos, has highlighted the problem of speedy early excavations, where much of the spoil from the tombs was not sieved and many important fragments lay in the spoil heaps where they have been found only in the twentieth and twenty-first centuries. Still to be seen today, however, the figure in dazzling white appears to wield some authority, presiding over the local workers in the pit, with three onlookers in familiar squatting pose, with additional clothing and possible bundles of lunch behind them. Judging by the general lack of activity, the photograph may have been taken during a break in the work or at the end of the day. Excavation in Egypt often begins around 6am, with a mid-morning break before fieldwork ends at around 2pm, thus avoiding strenuous physical labour during the hottest part of the day.

Investigations into the date of this double burial (F5) are unfortunately not aided by the description found on the corresponding tomb card. It simply states that the burial was found on November 16th 1908 by Abd el-Megid el-Kasan, the grave being 36"× 63", with a depth of 4' 'from the surface to bottom of grave'. The orientation of the grave is north-east to south-west, which is not remarkable given that from early times burials were not always strictly aligned to the four cardinal points, but had been aligned at the time of burial according to such factors as the sun's position in the sky at the given time of year. What is remarkable, however, comparing the burial photograph with the card, is that the card states: 'Only sternum, vertebra, and ½ pelvis [were found] on floor of N. corner' while two better preserved skeletons are visible on the photograph. This card, like all the others from the cemetery excavation, was signed by Edward R. Ayrton. The original glass negative is housed in a paper envelope which clearly notes it as burial F5, so there must a mistake on either the envelope or the tomb card, unless only a few bones were found originally and further excavation in F5 produced this double burial.

The exhibition catalogue for the el-Mahasna finds refers to 'Table A, Objects from the Predynastic Cemetery'. The catalogue describes burials of 'a well known type' from the Predynastic period, adding that bodies were 'occasionally' wrapped in mats of either animal skin or reed, or that 'in a few cases' the body was actually cut up before being placed in the grave; these include burials where the heads have been separated from the body at some stage prior to burial. Recently excavated examples include those from Adaïma and Hierakonpolis and it is also not unusual to excavate burials which have missing or displaced hand and feet bones. There is a tomb card for Cemetery F, Tomb 8, which was completed (the finder's name is not given) on November 16th 1908, and signed by Edward R Ayrton. The card contains a sketch of the burial pit in which the coffin was found, which is 5' long southeast to northwest and 4' wide in the southern end and 6' wide at the northerly end. The depth is noted as being 4' 5" and approximately 12" of loose sand above this. The pottery coffin is curiously described as empty and the dimensions of the coffin are given as 4' 4' long, 18" wide and 8" high. Looking at this photograph (labelled as being F8) the length is not impossible but there is an altogether more oval shape to the burial, so either the sketch is inaccurate, or the photograph and the card are of different graves. That the coffin is described as empty is also odd because this is not a description used purely for grave goods as other entries on this series of tomb cards include sketches of the position of the human remains. The burial that we can see in the picture is flexed, as we would expect from an early burial, although the construction of the top of the coffin makes it highly possible that it could be a good deal later – the coffin is also similar to types found in the Roman period.

This photograph is marked 'cem. F?' and when compared with the images of Cemetery F on previous photographs, it seems very likely that we are looking at the same expanse of land, but this time looking down towards the cultivation. The stark contrast of desert and fertile land is the same throughout the Egyptian Nile Valley as here. The primary tools of the trade, the same then as now, are the *faz* or *touriah*, of which at least two can be seen to the right and centre of the picture (perched on the workers' shoulders) and the baskets, one beside the foot of the man, ninth from the left. Much of the equipment is the same as today, with the exception of the baskets (known as *muktuf*s or *zambil*s) which are now often made from re-constituted tyres.

Grenfell and Hunt at Oxyrhynchus and in the Fayum

Dominic Rathbone

Bernard Grenfell and Arthur Hunt were pioneers in the discovery and publication of texts on papyrus from Graeco-Roman Egypt. Grenfell first visited Egypt in 1893/94 to work with Petrie at Koptos, and his first papyrological publications were of texts purchased by Petrie and himself. In winter 1895/96 he and Hunt began investigating abandoned Graeco-Roman villages in the Fayum, and in another four seasons from 1898/99 to 1902 they dug at a dozen village sites. The photograph heading this chapter shows them outside their tent in the Fayum, Grenfell to the left and Hunt to the right. In 1902 and 1902/03 they also dug briefly at el-Hibeh and nearby sites. In winter 1896/97 they had dug with great success at ancient Oxyrhynchus, where they worked for a further five seasons from 1903 to 1906/07. A combination of Grenfell's ill health and shortage of funds postponed indefinitely their planned return.

The aim of Grenfell and Hunt's expeditions, in common with others of that time and later, was to recover ancient texts on papyrus. They had little interest in the archaeology of the sites where they worked. They kept no systematic records and made no plans of their excavations, although Grenfell was preparing for publication an annotated map of the mounds at Oxyrhynchus which he never finished. However they were diligent in keeping the mummies, complete pots and objects of all types, from plough to haircomb, found incidentally by their workmen. The EEF distributed the objects assigned to it by the *Service des Antiquités* to institutions which had helped fund the expeditions. Hunt was also an enthusiastic and skilled photographer. Over 250 of his photographs survive which provide valuable evidence for the sites and finds and their working methods and conditions.

Grenfell and Hunt's fame rests on their achievements as papyrologists. They endowed the EES with the world's richest collection of papyri of around half a million fragments. They knew what texts they and their supporters wanted to find: first, early Christian writings, and second, lost masterpieces of ancient Greek literature. They sought out mummies in cartonnage hoping that it would be made of literary rolls, and they chose to dig at Oxyrhynchus because of its reputation in late antiquity as a fervent Christian centre. Oxyrhynchus gave them what they wanted. However, the vast bulk of their finds was of documentary texts, public and private, of every type, mostly in Greek, from the early Ptolemaic period to the Fatimid era. Papyrologists today draw on a century of academic experience and numerous works of reference and interpretation. Grenfell and Hunt were part of the small group of scholars who created that tradition. They worked tirelessly to decipher, interpret and publish the unparalleled range of texts they had found, and their numerous volumes set the gold standard in terms of quality and lucidity for papyrological publication. The EES continues to publish the series they started of *The Oxyrhynchus Papyri*. To date, through the efforts of several generations of scholars, some 5,000 texts have been published, making this the best published large collection in the world. The work goes on.

Alerted by working with Petrie to the potential of Graeco-Roman village sites in the Fayum, David Hogarth and Grenfell, soon joined by Hunt, began by digging at the site of Kom Ushim, ancient Karanis, from December to February 1895/96. Among other finds they discovered and cleared the south temple whose entrance is shown in this picture. The inscription on the lintel of the gate reveals that the temple was dedicated under the emperor Nero, on 7 July 64 AD, to the crocodile-related gods Pnepheros and Petesouchos. Hogarth planned the buildings they found. His private diary of this expedition also survives, and records the often difficult circumstances in which they worked.

In their 1898/99 season Grenfell and Hunt explored the mounds of Graeco-Roman villages in the north-west corner of the Fayum. These mounds were created by successive generations building on top of the detritus of their predecessors. The mound at Harit (Ihrit), site of ancient Theadelphia, seen here from the east in February 1899, with Grenfell and Hunt's encampment to the left, lay in the desert just beyond the expanding zone of cultivation. Local diggers had only exposed a small temple, and the few houses which Grenfell and Hunt excavated were largely intact. Today the site, surrounded by cultivation, is a flat carpet of potsherds with a few scattered remnants of Roman-period brick-and-concrete buildings.

Grenfell and Hunt also dug in the cemeteries adjacent to the village mounds in the hope of finding human mummies wrapped in cartonnage made out of old rolls and sheets of papyrus, as Petrie had at Gurob. In December to March 1899/1900 they worked at Umm el-Baragat, ancient Tebtunis, on behalf of the University of California. Their numerous finds from the site of the town included texts from the great priestly archive later excavated by an Italian expedition, but the cemeteries proved equally rewarding. Typically they used numerous workmen: at Tebtunis they began with 40 men, soon increased to 100 and then 140. The men dug with their hoes, the basic tool of the Egyptian farmer.

In a cemetery at Tebtunis 'one of our workmen, disgusted at finding a row of crocodiles where he expected sarcophagi, broke one of them in pieces and disclosed the surprising fact that the creature was wrapped in sheets of papyrus. As may be imagined, after this find we dug out all the crocodile tombs in the cemetery; and in the next few weeks several thousands of these animals were unearthed, of which a small proportion (about 2 per cent) contained papyri'. These papyri of the later second and early first BC included the archive of Menches, village-scribe of Kerkeosiris, which provides an unrivalled view of village society and Ptolemaic administration in this period.

On the southern edge of the town site of Tebtunis Grenfell and Hunt excavated part of a monastic complex. The room shown here re-used Middle Kingdom column capitals. The paintings on the wall in the shadow portray St Theodore Stratelates on a prancing white horse and another unidentified mounted saint (possibly St George); on the wall to the right is a line of robed figures holding chalices. The paintings have been dated to the mid-tenth century AD. Subsequent Italian excavations revealed another ancient monastery and two churches at Tebtunis.

In winter 1900/01 Grenfell and Hunt returned to the Fayum. One site which they examined briefly was Rubayyat (Kom el-Kharaba el-Kebir), ancient Philadelphia. It was subsequently thoroughly dug out by dealers and local farmers, whose finds included the huge Zenon archive which attests the town's development in the third century BC. Unusually for rural settlements in Graeco-Roman Egypt, Philadelphia conserved through to its abandonment in the fifth or sixth century AD the rectangular street-grid of its foundation under the Ptolemies. This photograph of a flat site by a canal (the line of trees in the background) may be the only extant view of the remains of Philadelphia before they were reduced to the present field of pebbles and potsherds.

The cemetery at Philadelphia was one of the main sources of the 'Fayum portraits', painted on wooden panels, which were inserted in the mummies of members of the local elite in the Roman period. These two portraits were found together by Grenfell and Hunt in February 1901, and are clearly by the same artist. They were painted in tempera, like most of the Philadelphia portraits. The hairstyle of the richly bejewelled woman resembles that of imperial women of the later second century AD. The boy wears a tunic with red stripes and a *bulla* round his neck, and his hair is plaited into a Horus-lock worn to the side. These are signs of high status and youth: at the age of 14 the lock would be cut off in a ceremony marking his entry as young man into the gymnasium.

In January-February 1901 Grenfell and Hunt dug at the sites of Dime and Quta (or Yakuta), ancient Soknopaiou Nesos and, probably, Heraklia, on the north side of lake Qarun in the Fayum. Among the finds at Quta was this damaged miniature marble head from a statuette probably of Alexander the Great. The Ptolemies promoted worship of the current and previous rulers of their dynasty, beginning with Alexander, and this head may have belonged to a statuette used for worship in a temple.

Grenfell and Hunt packed the finds from their excavations into wooden crates for ship-ment back to Oxford. Small objects were first put into cigarette boxes and biscuit tins (such as those which can be seen in the image on p.204) from their supplies. Transport from the remoter Fayum sites required the use of camels. The EES archives hold some notes in Hunt's hand which record the packing in 1901 of crates 5 and 6 (possibly the crates in this photograph) with finds from Soknopaiou Nesos and nearby, and 13 and 14 with finds from Philadelphia.

In their visits of March-April 1902 and January 1903 to el-Hibeh, Grenfell and Hunt dug in the Graeco-Roman cemeteries outside the north wall of the town, ancient An-kyron. Here too they found numerous mummies with decorated facemasks and other pieces similar to their Fayum finds. The cartonnage which they purchased and found was composed of Greek documents of the third century BC. In the second season they found some Roman-period portrait mummies, and also more decorated Ptolemaic wooden coffins, like those shown here, and some mummies of dogs dedicated to the cult of Anubis, chief deity of the neighbouring Cynopolite nome.

The ancient city of Oxyrhynchus lay on the west bank of the Bahr Yusuf (Joseph's Channel) some 180 km south of modern Cairo. Grenfell and Hunt first excavated there in 1896/97 and then for another five seasons from 1903 to 1906/07. The Bahr Yusuf, seen here looking north, is an improved secondary channel of the Nile which flows north along the western edge of the middle Nile valley. In the background are the canal-side orchards and some minarets of the village of Behnesa, to which occupation of the site had atrophied in the medieval period. The local fishermen, as this photograph shows, used distinctive reed rafts from which to fish. In ancient times the 'sharp-nosed' (Greek: *oxurhunchos*) fish was the chief deity of the region.

In the Roman and Byzantine periods the city of Oxyrhynchus had occupied an area at least two km long and one km wide, and had been adorned with fine public buildings and colonnaded streets. Long before Grenfell and Hunt arrived, virtually the whole site had been thoroughly dug out to recover building materials for re-use, and they found it a desolate plain scattered with mounds of the rejected detritus, as this view east across the site illustrates. In the middle horizon rises the minaret of the mosque of Zain el-Abidin (also visible in the view opposite, to the left), nowadays partly collapsed, whose base incorporates elements of the monumental eastern gateway of the ancient city leading to its port on the Bahr Yusuf. Just off to the right of the picture is where Grenfell and Hunt noticed traces of a substantial stone building which Petrie excavated in 1922 and discovered to have been a massive stone theatre, the biggest in Roman North Africa.

When Grenfell and Hunt realised that almost all the mounds of Oxyrhynchus contained fragments of texts on papyrus, they began more systematic excavation of them, although they left alone the mounds nearest Behnesa with only Byzantine to Arab material. Their favoured method was to cut trenches into the sides of the mounds, following the 'veins' of papyri. These trenches could go eight metres deep before reaching the damp layers where papyrus was ill preserved. Each year Grenfell and Hunt employed over a hundred local workmen, and their winter seasons had to end when the men began to drift back to agricultural tasks.

At the trench face, pairs of workers, usually a man and a boy, carefully dug out the detritus and sorted it for papyrus fragments. Wicker baskets were used to remove the spoil and to keep the day's papyri. Grenfell mostly supervised the digging while Hunt stayed in their base where he received and sorted the papyri and other finds preparatory to the evening's work of classification and preliminary decipherment. Hunt also took all, or almost all, of the photographs. His talent for photography is exemplified by this shot which neatly includes his own shadow.

Tombs of locally revered sheikhs were built on top of some of the mounds of detritus left from the recovery of reusable building materials from the site of Oxyrhynchus, and its south end came to be used as a cemetery. Grenfell and Hunt worked carefully round the tombs, one of which they repainted. This view of the mound capped by the tomb of Abu Teir shows the result of their digging: the core is left, surrounded by ridges where the spoil from their trenches had been dumped. Their working procedures left plenty to be found by the Italian excavations of 1910-14 and 1927-34 and other diggers. No accessible mounds now remain on the site, but since the 1980s there has been new archaeological work in the *oxurhunchos*-fish and human cemeteries and on the traces of the urban plan.

In their first season at Oxyrhynchus in 1895/96 Grenfell and Hunt started on the Graeco-Roman cemeteries to the west of the town site, but after three weeks gave up when they discovered they were permeated by damp and had already been plundered, and that most bodies had not been mummified. In a few graves they found figures like these, which had been tipped back into them, from a third to half life-size, carved from single blocks of limestone and originally painted in bright colours. The context, style, clothing and hairstyles of these figures, which had probably been placed in small cult chapels above the graves, suggest that they date to the third century AD, the peak of Oxyrhynchus' prosperity.

Among the finds of the first season at Oxyrhynchus in 1896/97 was this fragment of a collection of sayings of Jesus, written in Greek around AD 200 (*P. Oxy.* I 1). Fragments of two other third-century copies were found in the second season there in 1903. Grenfell and Hunt rushed out a publication of the first text of the sayings in July 1897 as a pamphlet which included a prospectus soliciting subscriptions to establish a fund to excavate and publish papyri, and later that year the Graeco-Roman Branch of the EES was established. They also re-published the text as no.1 of the new series of *The Oxyrhynchus Papyri*. The collection of writings found at Nag Hammadi in 1945 included a complete fourth-century version of the text in Coptic which enabled identification of it as the Gospel of Thomas. The papyrus is now in the Bodleian Library, Oxford.

On 13 January 1906 Grenfell and Hunt hit on a particularly rich dump of torn papyrus rolls with copies of works of Greek literature. A few fragments found that year were joined by larger pieces in 1907 which revealed some 400 lines of a second-century AD copy of Sophocles' *Ichneutai* ('Trackers'), still the only known example of a satyr-play by Sophocles. In it the chorus of Satyrs track down the stolen cattle of Apollo to a cave where Hermes, the thief, is inventing the lyre which he then presents to Apollo. Sophocles' play inspired Tony Harrison's *The Trackers of Oxyrhynchus*, first performed at Delphi in July 1988, in which Grenfell and Hunt take the place of the two deities. The papyrus (*P. Oxy.* IX 1174) is now in the British Library.

P. OXY. 1911

Most of the papyri found at Oxyrhynchus by Grenfell and Hunt were public and private documents of the second century BC to tenth century AD. Several of the mounds of rubbish produced texts mainly of the Byzantine period, including a large archive relating to the estate of the Flavii Apiones, more of which was found by the later Italian excavations. This was one of the leading families of the Byzantine empire: one member, Apion I, was a trusted official of the emperor Anastasius, and his son, Strategios II, was prominent under Justinian. The 250 and more texts so far published range in date from the mid-fifth century to AD 622. They include rent rolls, of which this is one (*P. Oxy.* XVI 1911) dating to AD 556/7, contracts with rent-collectors, receipts by tenants for parts of irrigation machines and so on, and tax accounts. The nature and management system of the estate and its role in the public administration of the region are matters of continuing scholarly debate because it is the best attested estate of the Byzantine world.

Deshasheh, Dendereh and Balabish

Andrew Bednarski

The sites of Deshasheh, Dendereh, and Balabish do not readily spring to mind when EES field-work is mentioned. Even *Excavating in Egypt*, the history of the Society's first hundred years' work, gives only cursory information about these three sites, choosing to concentrate on EEF/EES work elsewhere. Such a reality is not very surprising, given the impressive finds, and far-reaching repercussions, that were the result of the Society's efforts in other locales. Yet despite the lack of attention that the Society's efforts at these burial sites have received, they remain important to the history of the EES, and to our general understanding of Egyptian civilisation.

In 1897 Flinders Petrie undertook a survey of the west bank between Minya and the Fayum. His goal was to record all of the town and cemetery sites, what he refers to as 'the real work of an Exploration Society', within the ninety mile expanse. After leaving the site of Behnesa (ancient Oxyrhynchus) to Bernard Grenfell and Arthur Hunt, he turned his attention to the site of Deshasheh where his work concentrated on the excavation of 150 Old Kingdom tombs and led him to develop his 'new race' theories. Upon arrival at Deshasheh Petrie purchased 10,000 mud bricks and then left to fetch his belongings, entrusting a boy to have the huts in which he would live and work built, returning four days later. Petrie described the site as a plain, gently rising from the cultivation for approximately two miles. At the limit of the plain was a limestone plateau of approximately eighty feet in height, containing tombs of various forms. The main focus of the season was to copy the scenes found within these sepulchres. To this effect, Petrie opened about 150 tombs.

The following winter, after his marriage to Hilda Urlin, Petrie returned to Egypt with a permit to excavate at Dendereh. He arrived at the site after a horrendous boat journey with his new bride, a trip far from the ideal honeymoon experience. Petrie had decided Dendereh would be worthy of investigation for two reasons: the town was an as yet unexplored Nome capital; and the cemetery promised to shed light on the First Intermediate Period, a segment of history still regarded as a 'dark age' in the record of Egypt. The cemetery is located on a slope of desert behind the Ptolemaic temple's enclosure wall, stretching for approximately a third of a mile up to a boundary bank. While Petrie mentioned its pillaging in modern times, he also happily noted the relatively minor archaeological impact that this thievery had upon the site. He began his work by excavating the cemetery's animal catacombs and, once cleared, they served as sleeping quarters for his workers from Quft. After his season, Petrie concluded that Dendereh demonstrated a continuity of civil life in Upper Egypt from the Old Kingdom through to the Middle Kingdom, helping to illuminate a little known period of Egyptian history.

A small chronological leap forward brings us to 1915 and the Society's work at Balabish. The site was excavated by Gerald Wainwright, a British archaeologist trained over many seasons by Petrie, for the American Branch of the EES, and was the only excavation undertaken by the Society during the First World War. In the published report Wainwright tells us that the Society had been granted a special concession in order to procure objects for a small group of American museums. More important to the excavators, however, was the discovery of a small group of Pan Graves found on desert promontories at the end of the site nearest the cultivation. Although the work at Balabish is probably one of the Society's less well-known excavations, the evidence it provided for the presence of Pan Grave culture in Egypt remains highly significant.

The objects above present us with some of the tools used by the ancient workmen who carved out the tombs at Deshasheh. Found within two unfinished tombs, these tools included wooden mallets, chisels, baskets and cord used to remove gravel. The discovery of these objects presents us with an answer to the logistical problem posed by the fact that the Egyptians often buried their dead at a fair distance from where they lived. 'Had the town been near the cemetery the men would not have left their tools behind, and if left by chance, they would have fetched them; it rather appears that the town was so far away...that each day they hardly thought it worth while to go up to fetch the property'.

Two of the tombs explored at Deshasheh by Petrie were of a father and son, Nenheftka and Nenheftek, who he believed were the Fifth Dynasty descendents of an official buried at Saqqara. These statuettes of Nenheftka and his wife Neferseshemes were found amongst the remains of nineteen figures in the father's *serdab*. All but two of the figures found had been wilfully damaged in antiquity. Vexed by this situation, Petrie wrote: 'How it should come about that the chamber should be ravaged, the heads broken off, and the bodies scattered in fragments, and yet the two large heads be saved absolutely perfect, is a mystery. How a head should have been picked up and laid in the recess, without a single bruise or scrape, seems impossible in view of the violence'. This tone of frustration reminds us that the full history of a site can often never be fully reconstructed.

During his exploration of the graves at Deshasheh, Petrie found that nearly half of the discovered bodies had been dismembered, with some body parts wrapped individually before the whole was reassembled for interment. He concluded that this practice stemmed from cannibalistic ancestry, publishing a discussion on this topic, disputed by the American Egyptologist George Reisner, in the *The Contemporary Review*. Margaret Drower's biography of Petrie claims that the skulls found at Deshasheh, coupled with crania measured from Behnesa, were used by Petrie to support his notion of a 'new race' entering Egypt early in its history and displacing the indigenous population. Dividing the human remains from Deshasheh into two broad categories, intact and dismembered bodies, Petrie undertook a detailed examination of the body parts. He concluded that there was no special type of burial associated with the intact bodies, as some had been found with coffins, some without, some contracted, others extended. His study of the dismembered bodies led him to conclude that there were no differences between customs, view of property, or position in life between the groups. In his examination of the Deshasheh skulls, however, he found evidence to support his 'new race' theory, and to relate his findings to the study of anthropology in Great Britain: '...the perfect bodies were better nourished and superior in ancestry, and so starting from a finer basis they did not need so much individual growth. The cut-up bodies had a poorer ancestry, and required more personal skull-growth to make up for that. This is analogous to the Cambridge result, that men who afterwards take honours begin with a better skull than passmen, but grow less actively during their college-life'.

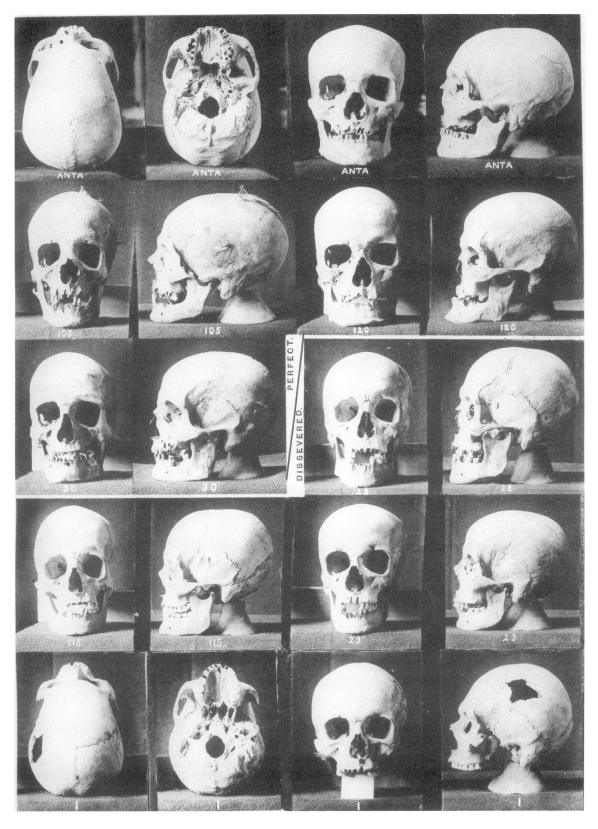

Married in her travelling clothes in 1896, Hilda Petrie was immediately whisked from the ceremony to Egypt. The eventual journey to Dendereh, which involved a particularly difficult trip on a filthy cargo boat, has, as Miss Drower describes, 'gone down in archaeological legend as "The Petrie's honeymoon on a coal barge".' Despite the hardships that surround archaeological work, however, Hilda Petrie took to life on an excavation immediately. She proved a valuable asset to Egyptian archaeology: assisting Petrie with field-work, accompanying him on all of his Egyptian excavations, raising funds for research, and publishing two works independently. This image shows her descending a ladder during the excavations at Dendereh and on p.231 she can be seen outside their house at the site.

In publishing material from Dendereh Petrie was faced with a dilemma common to Egyptian archaeology: on the one hand is the desire of the excavator to make as much data as possible available to researchers through publication; on the other hand are the financial constraints involved in publication. How does one decide which objects will prove valuable to future research and should, therefore, be made publicly available? As a solution, Petrie split the enormous amount of material found at Dendereh, much of it inscriptional, between two publications. The first was the creation of the usual EEF edition, issued to all subscribers, and containing material thought to be of general interest. The second was a smaller edition of 250 copies. Petrie proudly claimed that this course of action saved '...some two hundred pounds in cost, without – it is hoped – sacrificing any of the usefulness of the publication'. Despite this ingenious solution, Petrie was still unable to publish all the stelae and blocks at large scale. These three blocks from the Sixth Dynasty tomb of Senna, for example, were reproduced at a very small scale in the volume where the finer details of the hieroglyphs and relief work were not visible.

Unfortunately, in his desire to publish the Dendereh material as comprehensively as possible, Petrie created another quite different problem as the pages of the Dendereh publication are filled with images of photos that had to be substantially reduced. As a result, the detail of the recorded objects is, at times, lost to the viewer. One example of this occurrence is the reproduction of this pair statuette of Mentuhotep and his wife Nefermesut. Petrie describes the piece as 'excellent work and admirable in the power of its expression'. Unfortunately, any such evaluation is difficult when using the original publication.

Similarly, the figure of Atsa from the mastaba next to that of Mentuhotep, was originally reproduced at greatly reduced size. This statuette was found *in situ* in a niche in
one corner of the burial chamber. The niche had then been plastered over, concealing
the statuette, and its discovery was only made by chance.

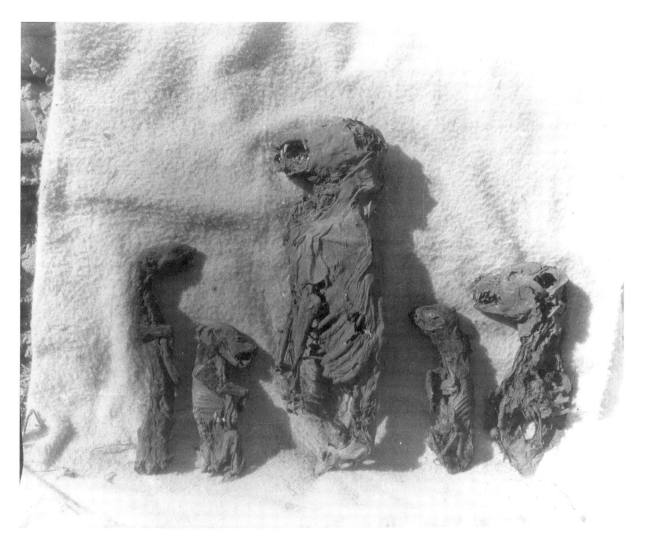

Not all work at Dendereh involved the excavation of human burials. The site's cata-comb of sacred animals was founded in the Twenty Eighth Dynasty and added to over centuries. Upon excavating two long chambers, Petrie discovered that they were full of dogs, some incomplete, others whole, dating to the Roman period.

General views of the site at Balabish, showing the location of the various burial areas through the ages. As with most sites in Egypt, these images also demonstrate how marked the transition is from cultivation to desert. Upon his arrival at Balabish, Wainwright found an extensive cemetery with burials dating to the Middle Kingdom, New Kingdom, and Coptic period. The site had been previously excavated by the Egyptian *Service des Antiquités* and frequently plundered by the local population, leaving only the parts nearest the cultivation unexplored. Despite this history of activity, however, it was hoped that Balabish might still yield types of pottery, as well as other objects of value sought by American museums, since this, as described above in the introduction to this chapter, was the main purpose of the excavation. Wainwright's work did not disappoint, and museum-worthy objects dating to the New Kingdom were procured.

This view of pay-day at Balabish, is typical of scenes on excavations in Egypt until fairly recent times. The director, Gerald Wainwright, sits behind a table with the workmen gathered before and around him, waiting to be paid. Most of the workmen have the tools of their trade, the hoe and basket, and wear traditional Egyptian dress, in contrast to the rather formal western clothes (including a tie) of Wainwright.

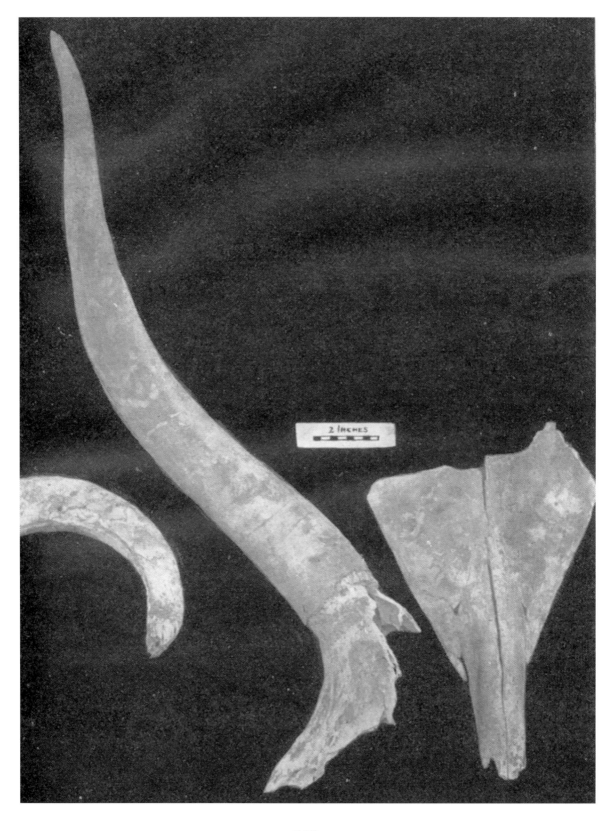

The scarcity of naturally occurring organic material in Egypt's desert offers excellent conditions for the preservation of organic material deposited below the surface. While this phenomenon lent ideological weight to the development of mummification techniques, it also results in happy historical accidents for excavators.

In the image above, we have several examples of stitched leather. One still contains pieces with animal hair stitched to other pieces of leather.

To the left are some of the most famous and distinctive finds in Pan Grave burials; the skulls of animals and horns, which were often painted. The Pan Grave people (contemporary with the late Middle Kingdom and early Second Intermediate Period) were from Egypt's Eastern Desert and their graves have been found mainly in Lower Nubia and Upper and Middle Egypt, though sherds of their distinctive pottery have been found as far north as Memphis. These people were famed equally as archers and nomadic cattle-breeders. The burial of horns relays nicely to us the Pan Grave people's desire to be associated with cattle.

In Wainwright's opinion, the most striking object from a particular group of artefacts was a vase in the form of a woman holding a lute. Dated to the New Kingdom, Wainwright describes it in the following terms: 'She wears only a girdle, and in the back view the hair is seen to be drawn back to a plaited pigtail, which forms the handle. The vase is made of alabaster, and that the workmanship is Egyptian is sufficiently evidenced by the treatment of the eyes and mouth. Nevertheless, the idea is foreign, and is no doubt connected with the zoomorphic art of Western Asia, and with the Greek rhytons'.

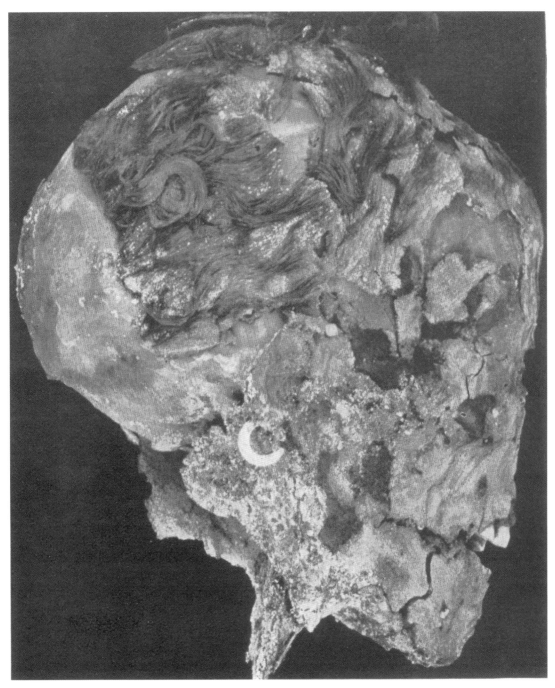

The head in this photo wears a penanular earring of hard, opaque, white stone in the right ear. The left ear contained two other stones, one of a similar material to that worn in the right ear, and one of carnelian. The stones were passed through holes in each of the ears. Such simple adornment may be easier for the modern viewer to relate to than the more popular images of funerary pectorals and gilded amulets.

The central object here is part of a female figure vase. In the same disturbed New Kingdom grave, B36, were found the four strange pottery covers, with animals sprawled over
them. Wainwright attempts to side-step the desire to classify them as canopic objects
when he states: 'As they are four in number, and are connected with animals, one would
suppose them to have come from canopic jars, but the animals do not agree with the
heads usually depicted on those covers'. To this writer, they remain a pleasant mystery.

Postscript

The Balabish excavation was the first to be published under the imprint of 'The Egypt Exploration Society' rather than the original name of 'The Egypt Exploration Fund'. With the change of name and the natural break brought about by the First World War, the 'Early Years' of the Egypt Exploration Society can be said to have come to an end. When fieldwork resumed in Egypt in the 1920s and 1930s EES excavations, led by Field Directors such as Oliver Myers, Henri Frankfort and John Pendlebury, would usher in a new era in Egyptian archaeology.

Photographic credits

Unless listed below, the images used in this book are copyright of the Egypt Exploration Society's and are held either in the Society's Lucy Gura Archive at Doughty Mews in London or, in case of some of the images from the work of Grenfell and Hunt, in the Papyrology Rooms at the Ashmolean Museum, Oxford. Many of the Grenfell and Hunt images have already been digitised and can be found on the website of the Oxyrhynchus Project: www.papyrology.ox.ac.uk/POxy/

The first stage of the digitisation of material in the Society's Lucy Gura Archive is now underway, with the scanning of around 14,000 negatives, many of which are large format glass plates, from the start of the Society's work in 1883 up to the 1930s. Progress reports on this important project will be posted on the Society's website: www.ees.ac.uk and included in future issues of the Society's colour magazine *Egyptian Archaeology*.

p.48 Copyright: Petrie Museum of Egyptian Archaeology. Negative No: PMAN 2702.

p.50 Copyright: Petrie Museum of Egyptian Archaeology. Negative No: PMAN 2683.

p.51 Copyright: Petrie Museum of Egyptian Archaeology. Negative No: PMAN 2680.

p.54 Copyright: Petrie Museum of Egyptian Archaeology. Negative No: PMAN 2682.

p.109 Drawing reproduced by permision of the Griffith Institute, Ashmolean Museum, Oxford.

p.227 Reproduced courtesy of The Bodleian Library, University of Oxford. Shelfmark: Oxford, Bodleian Library, MS. Gr. th. e. 7 (P).

Select Bibliography

compiled by
Christopher Naunton

The early history of the EEF (general)

Dawson, W R and E P Uphill, *Who Was Who in Egyptology* (3rd revised edition edited by M L Bierbrier, The Egypt Exploration Society, 1995).

Dodson, A '125 & still counting. Work of the Egypt Exploration Society 1882-2007' *KMT* vol.18, no. 2 (Summer 2007), 32-44.

Drower, M S, 'Gaston Maspero and the Birth of the Egypt Exploration Fund (1881-3)' *JEA* 68 (1982), 299-317.

Drower, M S, *Flinders Petrie: A Life in Archaeology* (2nd edition, The University of Wisconsin Press, Madison, Milwaukee and London, 1995).

Drower, M S, *Letters from the Desert. The Correspondence of Flinders and Hilda Petrie* (Aris & Phillips Ltd., Warminster, 2004).

James, T G H (ed.), *Excavating in Egypt: The Egypt Exploration Society 1882-1982* (British Museum Publications Ltd., London, 1982).

James, T G H, *Howard Carter: The Path to Tutankhamun* (2nd edition, Tauris Parke Paperbacks, London, 2001).

Moon, Brenda, *More Usefully Employed. Amelia B. Edwards, writer, traveller and campaigner for ancient Egypt* (EES Occasional Publication 15; The Egypt Exploration Society, London, 2006).

Petrie, W M F, *Ten Years' Digging in Egypt 1881-1891* (2nd revised edition, The Religious Tract Society, London, 1893).

Petrie, W M F, *Seventy Years in Archaeology* (Sampson Low, Marston & Co., London, 1931).

Rees, J, *Amelia Edwards, Traveller, Novelist and Egyptologist* (The Rubicon Press, London, 1998)

Rees, Joan, 'Petrie as Poet' *EA* 22 (Spring 2003), 18-19.

Naville in the Delta and at Ehnasya

EEF Memoirs:

Naville, E, *The Store-City of Pithom and the Route of the Exodus* (EEF Excavation Memoir 1; The Egypt Exploration Fund, London, 1885).

Naville, E, *The Shrine of Saft el Henneh and the Land of Goshen* (EEF Excavation Memoir 4; The Egypt Exploration Fund, London, 1887).

Naville, E and F Ll Griffith, *The City of Onias and The Mound of the Jew* (EEF Excavation Memoir 7; The Egypt Exploration Fund, London, 1890).

Naville, E, *Bubastis (1887-1889)* (EEF Excavation Memoir 8; The Egypt Exploration Fund, London, 1891).

Naville, E, *The Festival-Hall of Osorkon II in the Great Temple of Bubastis (1887-1889)* (EEF Excavation Memoir 10; The Egypt Exploration Fund, London, 1892).

Naville, E et al, *Ahnas el Medineh (Herakleopolis Magna) with chapters on Mendes, the Nome of Thoth and Leontopolis and an Appendix on Byzantine Sculptures with The Tomb of Paheri at el Kab* (EEF Excavation Memoir 11; The Egypt Exploration Fund, London, 1894).

See also:

Spencer, A J, 'The Delta' in James, T G H (ed.), *Excavating in Egypt: The Egypt Exploration Society 1882-1982* (British Museum Publications Ltd., London, 1982), 37-50.
Spencer, Neal, 'The great naos of Nekhthorheb from Bubastis' *EA* 26 (Spring 2005), 21-24.
Spencer, N with a contribution by Daniela Rosenow, *A Naos of Nekhthorheb from Bubastis. Religious Iconography and Temple Building in the 30th Dynasty* (The British Museum, London, 2006).

Petrie in the Delta

EEF Memoirs:

Petrie, W M F, *Tanis. Part* I. *1883-4* (EEF Excavation Memoir 2; The Egypt Exploration Fund, London, 1885).
Petrie, W M F, *Naukratis. Part* I. *(1884-5)* (EEF Excavation Memoir 3; The Egypt Exploration Fund, London, 1886).
Petrie, W M F et al, *Tanis. Part* II *Nebesheh (Am) and Defenneh (Tahpanhes)* (EEF Excavation Memoir 5; The Egypt Exploration Fund, London, 1888).
Gardner, E A and F Ll Griffith, *Naukratis. Part* II (EEF Excavation Memoir 6; The Egypt Exploration Fund, London, 1888).

See also:

Leclère, François, 'An Egyptian temple at Tell Dafana' *EA* 30 (Spring 2007), 14-17.
Spencer, A J, 'The Delta' in James, T G H (ed.), *Excavating in Egypt: The Egypt Exploration Society 1882-1982* (British Museum Publications Ltd., London, 1982), 37-50.

The Archaeological Survey

EEF Memoirs:

Newberry, P E, *Beni Hasan. Part* I (EEF Archaeological Survey Memoir 1; The Egypt Exploration Fund, London, 1893).
Newberry, P E, *Beni Hasan. Part* II (EEF Archaeological Survey Memoir 2; The Egypt Exploration Fund, London, 1894).
Newberry, P E, *El Bersheh. Part* I. *The Tomb of Tehuti-Hetep* (EEF Archaeological Survey Memoir 3; The Egypt Exploration Fund, London, 1895).

Newberry, P E, *El Bersheh. Part* II (EEF Archaeological Survey Memoir 4; The Egypt Exploration Fund, London, 1896).

Griffith, F Ll, *Beni Hasan. Part* III (EEF Archaeological Survey Memoir 5; The Egypt Exploration Fund, London, 1896).

Griffith, F Ll, *A Collection of Hieroglyphs. A Contribution to the History of Egyptian Writing* (EEF Archaeological Survey Memoir 6; The Egypt Exploration Fund, London, 1898).

Griffith, F Ll et al, *Beni Hasan. Part* IV. *Zoological and other details* (EEF Archaeological Survey Memoir 7; The Egypt Exploration Fund, London, 1900).

Davies, N de G, *The Rock Tombs of Sheikh Said* (EEF Archaeological Survey Memoir 10; The Egypt Exploration Fund, London, 1901).

Davies, N de G, *The Rock Tombs of Deir el Gebrawi. Part* I. *Tomb of Aba and Smaller Tombs of the Southern Group* (EEF Archaeological Survey Memoir 11; The Egypt Exploration Fund, London, 1902).

Davies, N de G, *The Rock Tombs of Deir el Gebrawi. Part* II. *Tomb of Zau and Tombs of the Northern Group* (EEF Archaeological Survey Memoir 12; The Egypt Exploration Fund, London, 1902).

See also:

Davies, W V, 'Djehutyhotep's Colossus Inscription and Major Brown's Photograph' in Davies, W V (Ed.), *Studies in Egyptian Antiquities: A Tribute to T. G. H. James* (British Museum Occasional Paper 123; The British Museum, London, 1999), 29-35.

James, T G H, 'The Archaeological Survey' in James, T G H (ed.), *Excavating in Egypt: The Egypt Exploration Society 1882-1982* (British Museum Publications Ltd., London, 1982), 141-59.

James, T G H, 'The discovery and identification of the Alabaster Quarries of Hatnub' in *Mélanges Jacques Jean Clère = CRIPEL* 13 (1991), 79-84.

James, T G H, 'The Very Best Artist' in Goring, E et al (eds), *Chief of Seers: Egyptian Studies in Memory of Cyril Aldred* (Kegan Paul, London, 1997).

Naunton, Chris, '"Careful Coloured Drawings": the watercolours of the EEF' *EA* 24 (Spring 2004), 7-9.

Willems, Harco, 'Fraser's 1892 map of Deir el-Barsha' *EA* 31 (Autumn 2007), 18-19.

Deir el-Bahari

EEF Memoirs:

Naville, E, *The Temple of Deir el Bahari: its plan, its founders, and its first explorers. Introductory Memoir* (EEF Excavation Memoir 12; The Egypt Exploration Fund, London, 1894).

Naville, E, *The Temple of Deir el Bahari. Part* I. Plates I-XXIV. *The north-western end of the upper platform* (EEF Excavation Memoir 13; The Egypt Exploration Fund, London, 1895).

Naville, E, *The Temple of Deir el Bahari. Part* II. Plates XXV-LV. *The ebony shrine. Northern half of the middle platform* (EEF Excavation Memoir 14; The Egypt Exploration Fund, London, 1896).

Naville, E, *The Temple of Deir el Bahari. Part* III. Plates LVI-LXXXVI. *End of northern half and southern half of the middle platform* (EEF Excavation Memoir 16; The Egypt Exploration Fund, London, 1898).

Naville, E, *The Temple of Deir el Bahari. Part* IV. Plates LXXXVII-CXVIII. *The shrine of Hathor and the southern hall of offerings* (EEF Excavation Memoir 19; The Egypt Exploration Fund, London, 1901).

Naville, E, *The Temple of Deir el Bahari. Part* V. Plates CXIX-CL. *The upper court and sanctuary* (EEF Excavation Memoir 27; The Egypt Exploration Fund, London, 1906).

Naville, E, *The Temple of Deir el Bahari. Part* VI. Plates CLI-CLXXIV. *The lower terrace, additions and plans* (EEF Excavation Memoir 29; The Egypt Exploration Fund, London, 1908).

Naville, E et al, *The XIth Dynasty Temple at Deir el-Bahari. Part* I (EEF Excavation Memoir 28; The Egypt Exploration Fund, London, 1907).

Naville, E, *The XIth Dynasty Temple at Deir el-Bahari. Part* II (EEF Excavation Memoir 30; The Egypt Exploration Fund, London, 1910).

Naville, E et al, *The XIth Dynasty Temple at Deir el-Bahari.* Part III (EEF Excavation Memoir 32; The Egypt Exploration Fund, London, 1913).

See also:

Davies, W V, 'Thebes' in James, T G H (ed.), *Excavating in Egypt: The Egypt Exploration Society 1882-1982* (British Museum Publications Ltd., London, 1982), 51-70.

James, Harry, 'Howard Carter and the EEF' *EA* 2 (1992), 3-5.

Abydos

EEF Memoirs:

Petrie, W M F and F Ll Griffith, *The Royal Tombs of the First Dynasty. 1900. Part* I (EEF Excavation Memoir 18; The Egypt Exploration Fund, London, 1900).

Petrie, W M F and F Ll Griffith, *The Royal Tombs of the Earliest Dynasties. 1901. Part* II (EEF Excavation Memoir 21; The Egypt Exploration Fund, London, 1901).

Petrie, W M F and A P Weigall, *Abydos Part* I. *1902* (EEF Excavation Memoir 22; The Egypt Exploration Fund, London, 1902).

Randall-MacIver, D et al, *El Amrah and Abydos 1899-1901* (EEF Excavation Memoir 23; The Egypt Exploration Fund, London, 1902).

Petrie W M F, and Griffith F Ll, *Abydos Part* II. *1903* (EEF Excavation Memoir 24; The Egypt Exploration Fund, London, 1903).

Ayrton, E R et al, *Abydos Part* III. *1904* (EEF Excavation Memoir 25; The Egypt Exploration Fund, London, 1904).

Naville, E et al, *The Cemeteries of Abydos Part* I. *The Mixed Cemetery and Umm el-Gaʿab* (EEF Excavation Memoir 33; The Egypt Exploration Fund, London, 1914).

Peet, T E, *The Cemeteries of Abydos Part* II. *1911-1912* (EEF Excavation Memoir 34; The Egypt Exploration Fund, London, 1914).

Peet, T E and W L S Loat, *The Cemeteries of Abydos Part* III. *1912-1913* (EEF Excavation Memoir 35; The Egypt Exploration Fund, London, 1913).

See also:

Dreyer, Günter, 'A Hundred Years at Abydos' *EA* 3 (1993), 10-12.

Kemp, B J, 'Abydos' in James, T G H (ed.), *Excavating in Egypt: The Egypt Exploration Society 1882-1982* (British Museum Publications Ltd., London, 1982), 71-88.

Wegner, Josef, 'Reopening the tomb of Senwosret III at Abydos' *EA* 30 (Spring 2007), 38-41.

El-Amrah, el-Mahasna, Hu and Abadiyeh

EEF Memoirs:

Petrie, W M F and A C Mace, *Diospolis Parva. The Cemeteries of Abadiyeh and Hu 1898-9* (EEF Excavation Memoir 20; The Egypt Exploration Fund, London, 1901).

Randall-MacIver, D et al, *El Amrah and Abydos 1899-1901* (EEF Excavation Memoir 23; The Egypt Exploration Fund, London, 1902).

Ayrton, E R et al, *Abydos Part* III. 1904 (EEF Excavation Memoir 25; The Egypt Exploration Fund, London, 1904).

Ayrton, E R and W L S, *Pre-Dynastic Cemetery at El Mahasna* (EEF Excavation Memoir 31; The Egypt Exploration Fund, London, 1911).

Naville, E et al, *The Cemeteries of Abydos Part* I. *The Mixed Cemetery and Umm el-Gaʿab* (EEF Excavation Memoir 33; The Egypt Exploration Fund, London, 1914).

Peet, T E, *The Cemeteries of Abydos Part* II. *1911-1912* (EEF Excavation Memoir 34; The Egypt Exploration Fund, London, 1914).

See also:

Catalogue of an Exhibition of Antiquities found by the Officers of the Egypt Exploration Fund at Abydos and at Sidmant, Etc., 1909-10 with an introduction by T. E. Peet and J. A. Dixon. (Egypt Exploration Fund, London,1910).

Petrie, W M F, *Methods and Aims in Archaeology* (Macmillan & Co. Ltd., London, 1904).

Randall-MacIver, D and A Wilkin, *Libyan Notes* (Macmillan & Co. Ltd., London, 1901).

Grenfell and Hunt at Oxyrhynchus and in the Fayum

The Graeco-Roman Memoirs series was inaugurated in 1898 with the publication of Grenfell, B P and A S Hunt, *The Oxyrhynchus Papyri* Volume I. The series has since included the publication of papyri from Tebtunis and other sites in the Fayum region, while the publication of texts discovered

by Grenfell and Hunt at Oxyrhynchus continues to this day. For further infromation on the care and publication of the Oxyrhynchus papyri (and more photographs of the site) see: www.papyrology.ox.ac.uk/POxy/

Grenfell and Hunt's own EEF reports on their work:
EEF Archaeological Reports: 1895-1896, 14-19; 1896-1897, 1-12; 1898-1899, 8-15; 1900-1901, 4-7; 1901-1902, 2-5: 1902-1903, 1-9; 1903-1904, 14-17; 1904-1905, 13-17; 1905-1906, 8-16; 1906-1907, 8-11.

See also:

Bowman, A K, Coles R A, Gonis, N, Obbink D, and P J Parsons (eds) *Oxyrhynchus. A City and its Texts* (EES Graeco-Roman Memoir 93, London, 2007).
Turner, E, 'The Graeco-Roman Branch' in James, T G H (ed.), *Excavating in Egypt: The Egypt Exploration Society 1882-1982* (British Museum Publications Ltd., London, 1982), 161-178.
Montserrat, D, '"No papyrus and no portraits": Hogarth, Grenfell and the first season in the Fayum, 1895-6' *Bulletin of the American Society of Papyrologists* 33 (1996), 133-76, pl.6-8.
Obbink, Dirk, 'Imaging Oxyrhynchus' *EA* 22 (Spring 2003), 3-6.
Parsons, P J, *City of the Sharp-Nosed Fish: Greek Lives in Roman Egypt* (Weidenfeld and Nicholson, 2007).

Deshasheh, Dendereh and Balabish

EEF Memoirs:

Petrie, W M F and F Ll Griffith, *Deshasheh* (EEF Excavation Memoir 15; The Egypt Exploration Fund, London, 1898).
Petrie, W M F et al, *Dendereh. 1898* (EEF Excavation Memoir 17; The Egypt Exploration Fund, London, 1900).
Wainwright, G A and T Whittemore, *Balabish* (EES Excavation Memoir 37; The Egypt Exploration Society, London, 1920).

Full bibliography of inscribed material from all sites mentioned in the text can be found in the *Topographical Bibliography of Ancient Egyptian Hieroglyphic Texts, Statues, Reliefs, and Painting* (series started by Bertha Porter and Rosalind L B Moss, assisted by Ethel W Burney, now edited by Jaromir Malek). For further information see: http://griffith.ashmus.ox.ac.uk/gri/3.html

Abbreviations used in the Bibliography

EA   *Egyptian Archaeology*. The Bulletin of the Egypt Exploration Society (EES, London, 1991 ongoing).
JEA   *The Journal of Egyptian Archaeology* (EES, London,1914 ongoing).